December 17, 2017

WHO'S YOUR COMMODORE

To Dany
Thank for your
support.

David Wardlow

DAVID WARDLOW

PAGE PUBLISHING, INC.
New York, NY

First originally published by Page Publishing, Inc. 2017

ISBN 978-1-64082-818-6 (Paperback)
ISBN 978-1-64082-819-3 (Digital)

Printed in the United States of America

A S THE AUTHOR OF THIS book with sixty years of life experience, I continue to challenge myself with the realities of life. I thought I would share a short insight into my findings.

If you like, I will continue, and if not, I will be retiring to my reality. We can always talk about me some other time. Quoting the words of Cheech and Chong, "Dave's not here!"

The intent of the story is to ask the question implied by the cover, its three occupants. They are asking you the question why life can be somewhat simple but has become more complicated, leading to more rules and regulations that seem to impede progress rather than improve the quality of any life. It might be time to recruit your input by reading this book. They are awaiting your reply.

Maybe it is time to engage with reality, not artificial intelligence. There is a belief that instinct, common sense, with education, equal intelligence and survival.

Life does run in parallel. What does this mean? We are in the wind and connected by water, which connects us to everything, making us one with nature.

It's time to remove some of the bull from our lives and get to the real problems.

Hope this can all make sense to you.

THIS A TRUE STORY OF my becoming a member of a Southern California yacht club. Later, I served on the board of directors and took a seat as a director through to the commodore's position of being in charge. The story expresses the frustration of the past with no direction and changing of the guard to a new and steady course. This is not about an exercise in seamanship but an exercise in "seniorship."

Seeing the climate of our current political system changing in this country made me see the need to tell this story. Most boards are governed by Robert's Rules of Order and their bylaws are supported by the SOPs (standard operating procedures) to keep continuity for their future.

Board differences are their types: nonprofit, business for profit, homeowner association, philanthropy, etc. Basically it's about solving and resolving their issues in a manner with control. They are not for creating chaos. I found it interesting that the personalities overshadowed this reality when all the tools for governing were in place.

My decision was to put this in writing to purge my soul, hopefully shedding light on what happens when in control versus being out of control.

This is a four-year journey. With this being said, I believe this plays to a much larger audience than just yacht clubs.

This is dedicated in fond memory to my commodore Sally Jo Giamo Hill and my mentor Eddie Calo.

CHAPTER 1

I HAD MY THOUGHTS OF WHAT a yacht club might be about. When you have not been a part of one, you would not really know. They would be good stewards of their waterways and its inhabitants, seabirds, mammals, fisheries, and certainly having a social atmosphere. Some yacht clubs have facilities and some do not.

So imagine you have joined a yacht club. After enjoying some time, you decide to run for a seat on its board. The board is the management overseeing most yacht clubs. A yacht club is a nonprofit social club, normally a 501 C7, which has federal and state guidelines. The specific and primary purpose for which a club is formed is to promote all forms of boating, to aid in the provision of facilities for the use of boats within along the coastline of California, to foster a closer fellowship for those using boats, to do such work and provide such facilities as is required, and generally to do all things that may aid in promoting interest in boats, boating, and related recreational activities.

You have succeeded being elected and served for two years, which is the usual commitment. You have served successfully as a director and vice commodore. It is now time to run for the board for a second term. The next position you would be running for is commodore.

You have mixed emotions about running because of other issues. Maybe things needing your undivided attention, which would interfere with your ability to perform at a level to oversee all that is expected as the commodore.

You receive a call from your treasurer. You have worked very closely with her, being you were the vice commodore, CFO of the yacht club. She states that she and her husband have postponed their cruising voyage until next fall. She says she would like to remain in her position as treasurer for your year as commodore.

I was very happy to hear that news and said yes. I asked if I might have a conversation with her. She replied, "Certainly, what's up?" I shared what was on my mind and the reasons I would rather not run for commodore. She certainly understood and was not trying to talk me out of it. She said, "Would you please run and get us headed in a good direction and do what you have to do. You are in the position to keep us going forward, and you have the members' support."

I thought for a moment and said, "OK, I will run." This was the morning of the day of elections to the board. I would have to be voted on to the board in order to run for the commodore position.

The election of the bridge officers would be the following month in October.

I thanked her for her advice and support. "I will see you tonight." I hung up the phone and began thinking of my presentation. It would be very important to make my case for running for the board including my intent to be the next commodore. It was equally important that they know I was not there to waste my time and get caught in the usual crap that seems to surface at meetings.

I had a briefcase I had never used. I packed it with three items I used in my business and a few other items I thought pertinent to this presentation. It was all coming together. I felt confident about this decision and my approach to the membership seeking their vote to continue on the board and ultimately become their commodore.

I think it is a good time to reflect and how all this came about. I was invited on a sailing vacation by a friend. He had been on this annual trip in the past. It was a group of guys from Minnesota and California. They chartered a sailboat in the British Virgin Islands. One of the guys had his captain's license. His experience came from sailing the Great Lakes. This was their way of getting away from their freezing winter for a week. I took advantage of this opportunity and we had a blast. We sailed during the day and partied at different locations at night.

After returning from the trip, I could not get the experience out of my system. I started looking for my own boat. The Channel Islands were just off our coast, so it all made sense to me. I had a friend who always invited me out on his boat, which was in the Channel Islands Harbor. He had a twenty-eight-foot Bertram. It was set up for fishing and diving. I lived an hour and a half further north and declined most of those invites. I was interested in a powerboat. The reason was I did not have a lot of downtime due to my work schedule. So getting to a location in a timely matter seemed critical.

I found a twenty-four-foot Renell locally that was sitting in a boat repair yard with a "for sale" sign on it. I stopped in and inquired about it. I made arrangements to meet with the owner. It was in the yard for repairs. The owner was an elderly retired man who loved fishing for salmon and anything else that would bite his hooks. His wife was very sick, and he felt he needed to let his boat go. He had brought it to this shop to fix all necessary items. I was shown the estimate for repairs, which totaled two thousand dollars. He was asking for 9,500 dollars. He stated that he would deduct the two thousand from his price or if I paid full price and he would guarantee all the repairs and anything else that was needed. "I don't want to sell you a lemon." I agreed on his full price but had to wait two months before all repairs were made.

When it was all said and done, the repairs came to a total of 2,500, which he paid in full as he promised with no further money from me. He was a man of his word. During my wait for my vessel, I got certified to dive and bought all the extra things needed to make this baby mine. I started diving with my friend off his twenty-eight-foot Bertram.

I finally got my twenty-four-foot Renell. I hauled it back to the farm and started installing my upgrades. Now it was time to get this baby in the water. The haul down to the Santa Barbara boat launch was about forty minutes. After thinking about it, Lake Cachuma was only twenty minutes away, so I decided to go there for the maiden voyage. I called a friend to come along and off we went. I had a three-quarter-ton two-wheel-drive Chevy Suburban to haul my boat. We arrived at the gate and told the ranger we were here to launch this boat for the first time. I paid the entry fee, and we headed to the boat launch ramp. The ramp was cement with grooves cut into it for traction, and it had a light coat of algae growing on it. I backed down the ramp and stopped and got out to remove the tie-downs. All looked good, so I got back in and started backing into the water. I gently touched the brakes, and the Suburban kept moving. The weight of the boat was pulling me into the water. We were now sliding backward. At this point, you could say the boat was towing me. Upon hitting the water, I was able to stop and considered the consequences of my dilemma. I looked at my buddy and said, "How bad do you want to go out into the lake today, considering I would have to call AAA to pull us out?" He agreed if we could get out now, that would be just fine with him. I backed up a little further and put the gearshift in drive and gunned it.

Fortunately, my tires were new and able to get to a dry spot to get the traction necessary to make our escape. After pulling back up into the parking lot, we boarded my vessel and popped open a beer and cheered to the adventure. We decided to have lunch and headed back to town. When returning to the ranger station, he said, "That seemed like a quick trip, how did it go?" I shared our escape. He laughed and returned my entry fee and said, "Better luck next time."

I was not pleased with myself with not succeeding with the maiden launch. I had overlooked the weight factor of the boat and my tow rig's capability. Instead of pondering too much and overreacting, I decided to use a little Yankee ingenuity. When I first got this horse farm, one of the last tenants had abandoned a 1975 four-wheel-drive Suburban. Mine was a 1985 Suburban. I had already pulled this unit into a barn and separated the body from the chassis. I had an idea of making a treadmill for horses from the parts. Instead it was now going under my Suburban. I would no longer fear the exiting of a boat launch again. Ten days later, out came a 1985 four-wheel-drive with a six-inch lift. Hooked that up to my boat, and off to Santa Barbara we went, never having that issue again.

Well, there were many great adventures on that boat, and I got many people interested in diving along with it.

Ten years later, it was time to make a change. I was storing the boat in between using it in an open-sided barn. Now this was a fiberglass boat, so there was no way for varmints to get in the boat, or so I thought. Well, a rat decided to drop in from the rafters above and boarded the boat, eventually filling the engine compartment with juniper branches. After cleaning this out for the second time, I decided I had better things to do and sold the boat. A month later, I realized how much being in the ocean was a part of me. I searched online and found my next vessel. It was in the Channel Island Harbor, which I was familiar with. This was a twenty-eight-foot Sundance made by Well Craft. It had twin screws, meaning two inboard engines. It was in a slip in a marina, and Anacapa Island was eleven miles away. I was sold. This provided me a vacation spot away from the ranch and a safer location from the pest at the ranch.

When you get a boat, you have to make it yours, so I started the improvements for its protection and my needs for comfort as well as it being utilitarian. When it was first purchased, the bottom of the boat had several months of growth, looking like a tide pool upside down. I had it professionally cleaned. A video showed the tide pool before and a slick desert afterward. The paint was in good shape. My girlfriend and I enjoyed many great weekends there. I thought if I was going to be spending time down there, it might be fun to get to know the area a little better. There was a yacht club not far from my marina. In fact, there were four yacht clubs in the harbor. This one was close and seemed to make the most sense.

One Sunday afternoon, the rear commodore was visiting her friends across from our boat. Our neighbor said we might be interested in joining, so she stopped by and said they had an open house that afternoon and we should stop by. I said we have company right now and have another engagement this afternoon but may stop by for a moment. She said that would be fine. We did go by and have a drink and looked around. They had a three-month trial membership, and that money would go toward a full membership if you decided to join. I quickly filled out the application and made the deposit. We were headed to Malibu for a friend's celebration of life. My interest in the club was they were a part of the White Sea Bass program. I

DAVID WARDLOW

had done something similar many years before. I was excited about the possibilities.

We started coming to the club to get a feel for the place. It seemed fun and friendly. The rear commodore's husband became my mentor and gave an introduction to the facilities. This was a self-help club, meaning the membership volunteered to do most of the work. We had two bartenders and one accounting person on the payroll. We did have a cleaning service to keep our facility clean.

We had a full kitchen for preparing meals for the members on Wednesdays and Saturday evenings. Our dining room was used for dining, dancing, and meetings. I started assisting in cooking meals so I could become familiar with the kitchen and the serving of the food.

I got on the parade of lights detail preparing our entry for the parade in our harbor in December. It was interesting working with these members. A member would donate their boat to be decorated with whatever the theme was for that year. There was a plan, and a person that was responsible to organize the execution and completion of our entry. I would drive down to participate in the construction of our float.

The theme would be announced by the harbor department in September, and the parade was the second weekend of December. It was quite a process. We worked every weekend on the project. This took about two months from start to finish. If you have not been to a parade of lights parade, it is very festive and entertaining.

After some time reading the dynamics of the work crew, I found it necessary to let them know I had three hours to work. I would appreciate if we would focus on the execution provided by the person in charge and less time contemplating the best way to do this. My point was accepted, and the work got done with less talk and more productivity. I hate wasting my time. Our hard work paid off, and we won all classes we qualified for. Good job!

During this time, there were many other functions at the club. Dining, dancing, fashion shows, etc. You could participate as much as you wanted. I finally decided it was time to take charge of cooking a meal for the members. Most Saturday night dinners were prepared by in-house cooking groups. On Wednesday nights, anyone willing could cook and put together a menu and crew. The food cost is reimbursed by the club; your labor, free. I decided to make my barbecued meatloaf, mashed potatoes, and green beans, with a spinach salad, amaretto, and ice cream for dessert. I prepared dinner for fifty people. There were no sign-ups for the Wednesday night meal. It was first come, first served. Usually thirty to thirty five show up. I figured the menu spoke for itself, and being a new member, people would be curious on how well I cooked. We served forty-eight people. It was well received. I did learn something. Does not matter how tasty your meatloaf is; ketchup and gravy are always asked for. Lesson learned!

Since that meal, I realized something was not the same between my girlfriend and me. I did notice she was not around offering help or interested on how it was going. No big deal. I did start noticing her car was in the club parking lot when I was working on the parade of lights project. She said she had met some new people and was busy enjoying their company. I knew she was not interested in our project.

Later she admitted she had met a guy at the dinner I cooked. Apparently they got into a deep conversation and one thing led to another. I had known this woman for several years before dating her. I was a bit taken back by the whole thing, but I kept my chin up and finished the project.

I had also gotten on the White Sea Bass program, and my day was Saturdays. The feeding and cleaning, and also keeping records of various situations like water temperature, mortality, food consumption, and overall health of the fish and conditions.

She ending up moving on with this guy and eventually moved to Hawaii. His forty-foot Swan was entered in the Trans Pac race. This was a race from California to Hawaii. It was captained and crewed by members of our club and flew our burgee. A week before the crew left, a fund-raiser was held to help with their cost. I donated a weekend at our ranch to help out. It was auctioned off at a final bid of $950. It included a dinner at the Hitching Post in Buellton for eight people and a dinner prepared by yours truly and a movie under the stars. Those who came still talk about that experience to this day.

After all that, I took a break and paid more attention to the ranch. My boarding numbers were down, and I needed more horses to meet the expenses. I had a facility for boarding retired horses. They were mostly sport horses that were turned out on irrigated grass pasture to live out their days. I usually had forty head, but it had dropped to twenty-five. About two months later, a new group was established.

I finally decided to get back to the boat and yacht club to find out what was happening there. My mentor was having some issue with his health and had been seeking answers to the problem. We were standing out on our deck one evening looking back into the club. I said, "You know I don't know about this yacht club thing."

He said, "You don't have to get to know these people—you just have to earn their respect and you will be just fine. There is something about you—I think you could help this club."

I said, "Oh no, I just wanted to get out of the weather once in a while and have a drink and meet a few interesting folks."

CHAPTER 2

I
T TURNED OUT HE HAD a brain tumor. They did the surgery in
which he survived but was not recovering well. We ended up
having a live wake for him at the club. He was very well liked
and respected. The attendance was outstanding. He and I were sitting by the fireplace, and he tapped me on the arm and said, "Are
you going to do that thing I asked you?" I looked perplexed for a
moment and realized he was referring to me running for the board. I
begrudgingly said OK.

He passed not much longer after that evening.

It was now July 2012. Someone came up to me at the club and
asked if I would run for the 2013 board. I did not even think; it just
came out as yes. I thought to myself, *Did I just say that?*

Afterward I was contacted by the nominating committee and
interviewed by phone by three members. They called again and asked
a few more questions. I was told they would approve of me being a
candidate. I was nominated before the membership and accepted as
a candidate for the 2013 board. I was told if I was truly interested on
being on the board, I would need to campaign. Well, that was not my
style. I did not know what people thought of me, but I would rely
on whatever that may be before worrying about it. I was voted in to
serve on the 2013 board in September.

Now around this same time, I had been seeing a very special
woman. We had met in passing, but it never went beyond that. She
invited me to a winemaker's dinner she had purchased at auction.
I agreed, and we hit it off. We started dating in late July. She knew
of my belonging to a yacht club, but she was not that interested.
Finally, one evening I told her I had been accepted to the board of

directors for 2013. I said it was for a two-year term. She was not too impressed. "How is that going to affect us?" she asked. I said it would not. There was a board meeting one Tuesday a month and six general meetings on Fridays through the year. She asked why I had run. I explained about my promise to my mentor before his passing and that I did have questions about how things are governed. She said she could live with that.

I had never served on a board before. Everyone said it was easy, but personal dynamics seemed to rule. So really it sounded like a test of your tolerance level. Mine was really short, so I guess I would see how it goes.

The bridge was voted in at the annual October meeting, which referred to electing the commodore, vice commodore, and rear commodore. After that meeting was adjourned, it was customary that we all retire to the bar and order one drink to be paid for by the incoming commodore. You could order anything you wanted but only one. This could get a little expensive sometimes. The price of fame, you might say. New board members were invited to sit in on the November board of directors meeting to get an idea of what went on. In the December BOD meeting, the outgoing commodore took the directors and their spouses out for dinner.

It was now time to serve as a director for a new year. Another task bestowed to me was serving as the leader of our men's cooking group. I was inducted in 2011 and was an apprentice for that year. The requirements to graduate and receive your chef coat was to crew on at least six dinners. Our group served at least ten dinners one a month and two special holiday dinners.

One of the dinners was the Navy Underwater Demolition Team and our coast guard. You could also crew a few Wednesday night dinners. I received my chef coat in 2012 and then asked if I would take the lead of our group for 2013. This meant finding chefs within our group to cook a dinner each month for that year, making sure this did happen and mixing up the menus. We also had two bonding meetings per year and a Change of Watch the following January. Sounds like a lot, but you just need to be organized.

The first dinner that we cooked was the Change of Watch dinner. It was usually the second Saturday of January. It was a sign-up dinner, and the cutoff was around one hundred. I took lead on this dinner. Change of Watch meant the outgoing commodore turned the club over to the new commodore, who introduced his new bridge members and board to the membership. The ceremony was not too long and there was dancing to a live band afterward. A fun evening for all!

It is important to understand the duties and responsibilities of the board members. The board supervises all officers, agents, and employees and sees that their duties are properly performed. Our board consists of nine directors including the commodore, vice commodore, and rear commodore.

The third Tuesday was the board of directors meetings. The commodore shall be the chief executive officer, shall have general supervision of the management of the club's affairs of business, subject to the advice and consent of the board, and shall act as chairman and preside at all board meetings. The commodore shall do whatever directed by the board and sign and execute all authorized bonds, contracts, and instruments in writing in the club's name. (S)he shall report to the board all matters within the commodore's knowledge that, in the club's best interest, must be brought to their notice. The commodore shall perform such duties as shall be assigned to the commodore by the board and shall be an ex-officio member of all committees except the nominating committee.

The vice commodore shall have such power and perform such duties as may be assigned from time to time by the commodore, subject to ratification by the board and/or the board and shall serve as the chief financial officer of the club. In the event of the temporary absence or disability of the commodore, the commodore's duties shall be performed by the vice commodore until the commodore's return or the removal of his/her disability. In the event of the resignation or death of the commodore, the vice commodore shall become the commodore immediately.

CHAPTER 3

THE REAR COMMODORE SHALL HAVE such power and perform such duties as may be assigned from time to time by the commodore, subject to ratification by the board and/or the board. In the event of temporary absence or disability of the vice commodore, the vice commodore's duties shall be performed by the rear commodore until the vice commodore's return or the removal of his/her disability. In the event of resignation or death of the vice commodore, the rear commodore shall become vice commodore immediately. A special meeting of the membership shall be noticed promptly to elect a rear commodore.

The bridge is also constructed with a secretary and treasurer, performing such duties as needed.

The commodore assigns a fleet captain, port captain, fleet surgeon, judge advocate, parliamentarian, chaplain, etc. The commodore assigns the vice commodore and rear commodore with all the committees they will oversee.

It seems like a lot to manage, but you need to work together to succeed.

Serving on the board for 2013 was not too labor-intensive. I was also serving as the food safety officer because I had a state food handlers and safety certificate. The commodore was a good communicator and stayed on course with the matters at hand. I basically listened and learned the first three quarters of the year, forming my opinions of what I was seeing. Growing membership was high on our agenda. Members were dying as fast as new ones were being signed up. We had a few disciplinary problems within the board. For the most part it was smooth sailing.

It was halfway through the year and it was time to pick a nominating committee for the 2014 board. I had another year to serve, so I volunteered to be on that committee. It would consist of two board members and three regular members. We were to contact names assigned to us and speak to those members who might be interested in running for the board, then make a final list and interview them.

We would then announce those candidates at the August general meeting. Any other member could be nominated from the floor when the commodore requested that. After that, each candidate had the opportunity to address the membership of their qualifications and desire for running. We had five candidates for four seats on the board. Four candidates were chosen to serve on the 2014 board at the September meeting.

October board meeting had come around, and I was having some serious thoughts about running for vice commodore. The candidate for commodore asked if I would run for vice commodore.

I did not give a final answer. There was no one to challenge the incoming commodore for the position. He had served as vice commodore for 2013 but was reprimanded for stepping out of line. I was aware of this and other actions I had been observing. If I was going to run for vice commodore, it was mainly to keep close tabs on this person. He was unaware of my concerns and supported me as a candidate for the position.

I spoke to my girlfriend about taking the position. She was not elated about it but would support me if I did. She did not want me to get engulfed in the problems of the club. I said I would do my best not to get to deeply involved. I did not want this to affect our relationship.

It was time for the last general meeting of the year and the elections to the bridge. The candidate for commodore had no challengers and was voted in. I was nominated from the floor to run for vice commodore. There were no contenders. I was voted in as vice commodore. The rear commodore position had no one running, so a new director finally accepted that position. After that, the meeting was adjourned. It was a custom to retire to the bar and get a drink paid for by the incoming commodore.

After the elections, the incoming commodore starts picking his staff. Sometimes the outgoing commodore takes the seat of a lame duck and lets the incoming commodore start taking over. I was observing the incoming commodore's actions. I was a bit disturbed by his approach to resolve issues. It appeared I might have my hands full. This individual came close to be commodore ten years ago and lost. I felt he was pushing a little payback for that. I just continued to observe and make notes of his actions.

I would share some of my observations with my gal, Sally. She just shook her head and said, "I told you so."

It was now December, around Christmastime. Sally was complaining of lower abdominal pain. She did not feel like eating much, but she loved to cook. She had seen her doctor, but he felt it was out of his scope and referred her to a specialist. The appointment was not until February 12. Not much could be done but wait. She was a very strong-willed person and hid the pain.

A notice was sent out by the YRUSC (Yacht Racing Union of Southern California) of their management seminar for new officers and directors. This seminar was about the management of a yacht club, your fiduciary duties and responsibility as a board member. In this presentation guidelines for 501 c7 nonprofit, ABC regulations, insurance coverage, labor code requirements, and food safety.

The seminar was held at Del Rey Yacht Club. The incoming commodore, vice commodore, rear commodore, and two directors attended. I found it very informative. The gentleman who was delivering his orientation had put much time into it. His presentation was in document form so you could reference it later when you needed guidance. I felt fortunate to be there and was given a better idea of what we had signed up for. We had no formal orientation at our club like this.

This document had a checklist, questions, and director's pledge, which I was unaware even existed. We had not been sworn in. This was a complete outline of what was expected of you as a board member.

We finished up the year with the Navy Underwater Demolition Team, coast guard, and celebrating Christmas and New Year's Eve.

Now it was January with the first Saturday being the commodore's cruise. The commodore went around and blessed our fleet with a prayer and a bottle of champagne. The Change of Watch dinner was the following Saturday. My menu was osso buco, polenta with golden raisins, baby carrots with caramel sauce, and a spinach salad. For dessert, fresh strawberries and whipped cream on fresh biscuits. I was still in charge of the men's cooking group so I would be the lead chef. Our Change of Watch was a week later on a Tuesday evening. Reservations reached 101. It was a real hit. I thought I would be happier cooking than observing the dinner.

We had our first meeting with the board. It was the third Tuesday of the month. The commodore laid out his plan for our future. He was unable to summit his budget. The meeting was short, and we were now off and running. All seemed pretty good.

The general meeting was the following Friday. It went reasonably well. When speaking as the vice commodore, I was blindsided by something that had been released to the membership via e-mail earlier that day I was unaware of the release. It was about a program we had started the year before at the members' request. After analyzing the data, it was apparent that it was not in our financial interest to continue. I stated that but was not prepared for the uproar. I held my decision and ground. I do not cave easily to chaos. After the meeting was adjourned, I had a few of the directors who understood what I was saying handle the disgruntled members. They were able to succeed at this in a one-on-one, making the outcome positive. Some people just overreact and can't hear the reality of what you are saying. It was my first and last confrontation with the membership. I made sure I had all and any facts available from that time on. I made sure the treasurer was as prepared as possible too.

CHAPTER 4

NOW LIFE GOT INTERESTING. THERE was a rumble that our accounting system was failing. Several changes were done at the end of 2013 going to 2014. I spoke to our accounting person, and she assured me she was on it and did not need any help. As it turned out, we did have a problem and she requested that a certain person come in and help with this matter. This person had helped in the past and we were not paying her, so I agreed. It turned out after two days, the problem was discovered, which had to do with the batching of credit cards. The commodore was informed, and when the problem was found, an e-mail was sent out explaining that credit cards had not been charged during January and early February and those charges were just now going to be showing up. I spoke to the commodore and said we were recovering the data in order to collect the funds. It might take a week. He apparently called accounting and started stirring things up the next day. That was no way to correct a problem. I received a call from accounting threatening to leave. I said, "Let me handle this." The commodore called me, and I told him to back off—it was being handled—and I stated the time factor. I hung up. This was Friday afternoon at 4:00 p.m. I am sorry—I do not work that way. He decided to call a special meeting of the board for Tuesday. I was furious. I had friends coming in for the weekend. What was this guy doing?

I thought about this over the weekend and discussed it with my weekend company. My friend was in business too and knew how delicate financial issues can be. Sally just shook her head like "I told you so." After pondering further on the issue, I decided to write a short but direct e-mail to the membership explaining further and asking for their patience. As vice commodore, I had access to sending e-mail to the membership. I received no replies. I did go down for the special meeting. I told my treasurer I would be running a little late but would be there. I wanted the meeting to be in session before arriving. When I went in, I would be able to read the room better.

I arrived and knocked on the locked door to the meeting. The treasurer let me in and locked the door. I heard directors calmly asking the commodore why this meeting was called. It was stated in the vice commodore's e-mail that a problem was found and being corrected and stated a time frame in that e-mail to the membership. The majority of the board members were all saying the same thing. The commodore said, "Well, I did not know the vice commodore was going to do that. He did not tell me."

A director said, "Well, he is the chief financial officer, are you going to let him do his job?"

I raised my hand so I could be recognized to speak. The commodore acknowledged me. I said, "I spoke to you last Thursday and clearly stated a problem had been discovered and was in the process of being fixed. The members had been notified by accounting. You interfered with the process after being told it was on the mend. So you ignored me. Then you call a special meeting." I reached for my phone and held it up. "This is my phone, I pay the bill. If you're going to call me and not listen to what I have to say, then I will not be answering your calls. There is no need for this meeting. You are just stirring things up." The majority of the board agreed and stated, "Let the vice commodore do his job and stop trying to micromanage." I said, "I am here to do my job, so let me." The commodore was quite taken back by the comments from the majority of the board. He thought he was in charge. I put out my hand and we shook on it. The meeting was adjourned. This happened to be the evening we were having our Change of Watch dinner for the men's cooking group. The commodore and three directors were in this group.

We did have our Change of Watch dinner. A new leader was dubbed and several new apprentices started their journey to become chefs.

This financial problem turned out to be a much larger problem but was handled without further incident. Too many changes had occurred at one time leading up to this mess. But we got it back online with patience and positive action.

That was just the beginning of our problems. There were always going to be disputes with members over whatever, but how would the commodore get himself involved? That should not be the way you conduct yourself. Unfortunately, that was the direction we were headed. I had no idea it could get this weird. Sally was right.

Sally's appointment finally arrived. She asked if I would go with her. I said, "I am right by your side." We arrived at the doctor's office in Santa Barbara. Sally was not sure what to expect. We were taken to an exam room. The doctor came in and asked some questions and did some palpation on her stomach. She said she wanted to do a few noninvasive tests. Sally went with her for a short time. Sally returned and said the doctor should be returning shortly. Sally did not know any more than that. The doctor returned and stated Sally would need surgery. It was suspected that she might have ovarian cancer. The doctor said she would check the surgery schedule and returned shortly thereafter. I just held Sally's hand. She was in shock but not registering the significance of the matter.

The doctor returned and said they had an opening on the fourteenth, which was two days away on Valentine's Day. I knew then this was very serious but did not show my concerns. The doctor made it out that this would be exploratory unless they found something. We left the office and stopped off at Cold Springs Tavern for a bite to eat. I could tell Sally was a little confused of what just happened. I kept the conversation light. We returned back to Sally's place which was across the street from the ranch. She told her landlords of what had been said. She then started making plans to pack for this trip. She was to be there at 6:00 a.m. on Thursday to check in etc. She refused to let me drive her. Her friend, the landlady, drove her down and made sure she got signed in and everything went well.

I was told not to worry and she would let me know how it went. Her friend stayed until about 1:00 p.m. I fed the horses early and went down and sat in the waiting room. She was in surgery.

It was estimated to take about four hours. The door opened, and a male nurse said, "Mr. Hill?" I raised my hand. It was not my name but Sally's married name. When she saw me, she was surprised. She was heavily sedated, so she could not be mad. The nurse moved her to one part of the hospital then realized she was supposed to be going to ICU. Glad I was there. We finally got her settled, and I just held her hand until she fell asleep. I checked in with the nurses on visitation and made arrangements to return. I hate being in a hospital.

I went at least once a day. Sally was not happy that I would drive down, but I told her she would have to get used to it until she was released. I stopped in most every day. On the fifth day, she was moved to her own room to recover. I visited and just tried to get her to cooperate with the nurses. She wanted out, but there was a protocol you needed to follow. Her doctor told her the operation went well but she would have to do chemotherapy within the next six weeks. Sally was finally released and started the mending process. She was happy to be home. I made meals, and we just hung out.

CHAPTER 5

I RECEIVED A PHONE CALL FROM the office stating a member who had paid his dues in full of $1,000 had stopped payment on his check. I asked why, but she did not know. She called this member, and he stated he had been confronted by another member while in the yacht club bar about losing money on a dinner in which he was in charge of. The altercation was in front of his fiancée.

This upset him, and the information this member had was not supported with all the facts. The facts would only be known by me and the commodore. So someone leaked out this misinformation, which caused this to happen. I asked the treasurer to call him and see if there was anything we could do. It had been stated that if he brought this to the board's attention, we could help resolve this. His answer was, "The board does not care." I e-mailed him and voiced my concerns and said I would handle this and get back to him. He appreciated this but said he would not be returning until next year. I said that would be fine and I would get board approval so there would be no penalty fees considering the circumstances.

I received a phone call at 8:45 p.m. on a Sunday evening from the commodore. I let it go to voice mail and decided to wait until morning so not to disturb my evening. Turned out that was most appropriate. The call started out, "You better get your ladies in line." There was something about them embarrassing him at the Midwinter's Award Ceremony. We hosted the Midwinter's Race over the weekend. I asked if they needed help. He said he had it covered and the rear commodore was really in charge since it had to do with boating. It was his responsibility to make sure all went well. This would have been his first event for the year. The racing event went as planned. It was the awards setup that took a turn for the worse. I decided to call the ladies first before responding to the commodore. I called the treasurer who was one of the ladies. When asked if he might be able have the area ready for the award ceremony, the commodore was not very accommodating which led to the outburst from my ladies for his reaction to this request.

The person representing the SCYA (Southern California Yachting Association) who was there to present awards was being disrespected by the commodore. He was being called out for his actions by these two ladies. I told her the commodore left me a message last night complaining about being checked for his actions. I asked, "Why did you not call me?" She said it was embarrassing and she did not want to bother me. I asked, "Where was the rear commodore during this time?" He went home after the race. I called the other lady and she supported what the treasurer had said about the incident. I did call the staff commodore from SCYA who was present. She said it was an unfortunate experience but did not want to say more. Another director had called her. She told him that it was not worth getting upset about. We felt embarrassed by his actions.

I decided to write a letter to the commodore expressing my disbelief of his actions representing our club as the commodore, including my thought of how he might consider stepping down as the commodore. Barely two months into the year under his leadership and this was what we were getting. I was certainly not interested in his position, but his present course was not in the best interest of the club.

I received your phone message at 8:45 last night and reviewed it this morning. After a few phone calls to the parties involved, I have come to the following deduction on the matter. I had wished I was offering you an apology for the ladies' actions yesterday, but after hearing more on that situation, I find yours totally out of order. Especially being an officer of the Bridge and the ambassador for the yacht club. Refusing to move chairs for the sake of a photo shoot to the chairperson of the SCYA and we are the host club is absolutely ridiculous. He was telling her to move the chairs herself. This tells me you do not care to conduct yourself in a caring and responsible manner. It was stated that we should not be bother hosting this in the near future. I hope we do not lose our sponsorship over this matter. This is not who we are as a yacht club.

Furthermore, I asked if you needed help with the food. You said you had plenty of bodies.

Come to find out you had one person in the kitchen to contend with preparing the food. You were next door at the museum. You should have had someone covering you. And asking racers to buy the food for which they had paid for that was included in the entry fee. What are you thinking?

Good grief, I do not understand your reasoning. You brought this upon yourself. You called me on this matter. I talked to the treasurer and the other lady. They said the circumstances were very embarrassing and did not want to bother me.

You know you were called out on your micromanaging by the majority of the board last Monday. You were also informed of the decent among some members and a rumor you would not make it to Opening Day as the commodore. Where do think this is all going if you do not get it together? You asked for our help last Monday and we said yes. We shook hands on it.

You are not getting the gravity of the situation.

As a friend and a fellow board member, I am going to offer you some advice. I personally do not see you changing. It is just who you are. If I were you at this moment, I would consider doing something like one of out past commodores. The circumstances were totally different but justified. You should resign due to a pending health issue and save face. You would still get out as a commodore. If you continue on the path you're on, it cannot be good.

Best regards.

I received no response to my correspondence to the commodore. I decided to look over our bylaws for some guidance to this problem. The bylaws of a yacht club are written to provide a strict guideline for governing that club. I did find a section that offered a solution to this problem. Certainly challenging, but I believed it was necessary. It would ultimately be up to the board to make that decision.

I decided to make a formal complaint against the commodore at the next board meeting. I spoke to my treasurer, who is also a lawyer. She agreed that following the bylaws as it is stated could help resolve this issue.

It was February and the evening of our second meeting of the year. Before the meeting, I asked to have a conversation with the rear commodore. I spoke of the issues I felt needed to be addressed about the commodore's actions. I showed him the formal complaint and asked if he would address this to the board in a closed session. He did not agree. I spoke to another director who was privy to the activities of the commodore. He said he would call for a closed session at the end of our regular meeting and address the board with my written complaint.

The meeting was called to order. We did the Pledge of Allegiance and called roll call. The meeting went fine. When the meeting was coming to an end, the director called for a closed session stating he had received a written complaint from a member which needed to be presented to the board. The complaint was read, pointing out two different issues involving the commodore's conduct. This was a rare case. Most complaints involved member disputes between one another. It was rare to be reading a complaint that involved a board member. When a complaint is presented to the board, the action taken is to notify the individual who is named in the complaint. They have seven days to respond in writing about the accusations being stated in the complaint. In this case, the person who the complaint was about was present.

The commodore started defending himself about the complaint and stating his side of what happened. This continued for several minutes. It was stated by more than one director that he should not say another word. "Get your thoughts in order and in writing to be submitted within seven days to the board. If you continue talking, we might have to vote on this tonight." He finally surrendered, and we closed the closed session and then adjourned the meeting.

At the end of seven days, a special meeting was called by two directors. It is stated in the bylaws that the commodore or two directors can call for a special meeting forty-eight hours before said meeting by electronic notice. This is what was done. The day before that special meeting, the commodore decided to call a meeting before our meeting. Ours was called for 6:30 p.m. He called a special meeting for 6:00 p.m. His agenda was to fill the vacancy due to the resignation of a director because a director stated he was quitting. No formal resignation had been presented to the board.

The special meeting requested by the commodore was called to order at 6:11 p.m. Present were the commodore, rear commodore, two directors, secretary, judge advocate, and the incoming candidate for director. Absent were four directors and the director in question. Since this meeting was called under the forty-eight-hour rule, the directors in attendance were there without protest and waived the notice requirement. A motion was made to accept and seconded and passed unanimously. The new director was introduced and accepted. A director made the motion to accept the interim director, pending confirmation at the March BOD meeting.

Approval was unanimous. Meeting adjourned at 6:22 p.m.; minutes were by the secretary.

The next special meeting was to start at 6:30 p.m. The vice commodore and three directors arrived at that time. Waiting at the table were the commodore, rear commodore, two directors, judge advocate, secretary, and the interim director. We were told what they had discussed at the meeting and that the director had been approved as interim and would be confirmed at the March meeting.

It was stated that meeting had no quorum, and how could this be considered a viable action when there had been no formal resignation of that director?

It was time to call our meeting to order. It was met with quite a lot of hostility. The commodore said he would preside over the meeting. The director who called the meeting along with me stated he would be the chairperson over the meeting. The judge advocate said, "You can't do that." The bylaws pertaining to this were read and they still would not allow us to open the meeting.

Tempers were running high. The interim director stood and said to the commodore, "If I were commodore, I would call the police right now and have these people escorted from the building." I thought to myself, *That is going to look good in the local police blotter.* We were considered by some as being the happiest yacht club in the harbor. After much commotion, I raised my hand to get the floor. When I was recognized, I said, "This is too bad and I just want to get the truth of the matter out. You obviously don't care." The judge advocate said, "Yes, we do!" I said, "Bullshit," and stood up, threw some papers down, and walked out of the room. One of the directors quickly grabbed those papers and came downstairs looking for me. I had already left the building and was in my car heading back to the ranch. At that point, I did not care anymore and turned the music up and enjoyed the ride home.

It is an hour-and-fifteen-minute drive if there are no problems. I received a few updates from directors stating the meeting never got opened. That one director grabbed the papers I threw on the table. It was my resignation and names of those who might feel like joining me. This was not seen by anyone else other than the director who grabbed them. The question presented to me was if I was going to resign, would they follow? If I would decide to stay and continue to take the lead, they would support me. I answered by saying, "Now that we know how they want to play, we will have to build a better strategy. I am not happy about the good old boys winning out. The March board meeting is three weeks away. Let's lay this at rest at the moment."

CHAPTER 6

I T WAS NOW MARCH. NOT much had been happening in a negative
way. It was time for the board meeting. Other than the board,
the judge advocate was present along with the commodore's wife,
a close friend of his who was a member of the club, and the interim
director. The meeting was called to order—Pledge of Allegiance to
the flag and roll call. The commodore once again was trying to introduce the interim director for ratification. The director addressed the
board. He would consider accepting but was concerned that a rumor
has risen that we may have made a decision he was not involved with
and he would not want to be implicated if that surfaced. He stated he
had heard rumors but he did not know the fact of what he has heard.
It was stated to him we have no idea what he was referring to, but the
point was the director in question of resigning had not done so in
writing, therefore he was wasting our time and his breath. It was next
stated by a director that he had spoken to this director in question
and informed him he could take a leave of absence, up to 120 days,
as long as the board approved it. This is what that director decided to
do. His mother had recently passed away and he was responsible for
dealing with all of that, and he was thinking of resigning, not realizing he would be able to take a leave of absence to handle those issues
and return afterward. It was duly noted that the commodore's wife
was leaking out information from the closed session in defense of her
husband. This director's friend's wife was accusing him and the board
of railroading the commodore. With the director taking a leave of
absence, we officially did not need an interim director. That interim
director walked out of the room with nothing else said.

Once that was settled, the commodore got off his high horse and settled down to business as usual. The meeting went very well. Everyone was cordial and got down to business. When the meeting was coming to an end, it was obvious the commodore was getting a little nervous, not knowing what was going to happen next. The directors were looking at me to see where I wanted to go next. I felt the meeting went very well after we settled the director issue. I just nodded. "Let's give this a time-out and adjourn our meeting." The commodore was almost out the door when we were ready to adjourn the meeting.

I spoke to some of the directors after the meeting. I stated I had seen an attitude change once we shut the director's replacement down. Maybe the commodore was finally realizing he was not in charge. "We can do this together or not." They agreed and said, "Let's see what happens."

The drive home was a pleasant one. After arriving at the ranch, I felt it was time to send the commodore another written explanation and cc'd all board members, along with a copy of the director's and officer's presentation by the YRUSC. This was a reminder of what was driving me to hold the commodore accountable for his actions.

I did not want the board members to think I was just going to let this go. He never offered us his written explanation. No one was aware I had sent him the first letter or of its content.

To the commodore:

> I wanted to explain my actions in the decision of registering a complaint against you. My observation of you handling various situations persuaded me to step back and try making my own evaluation of the matters at hand. You really wanted to help the accounting person with an assistant. When I spoke to that person, she said I need to be left alone so I can concentrate on the financial problem. At that time, I did not realize the amount of interruptions she was experiencing from you and many others. It would be very hard

to focus. You called a special meeting on this matter but did not have enough information to make a decision. I explained to you that it would be better to approach me or the treasurer about anything you needed. Your presence only made the problem worse. After that, the accounting person could focus on the issues and she asked for help. There was a person who had assisted in the setup of the POS system a few years early. The problem seemed to be coming from the POS (point of sales) system. I approved her request. The person of interest was volunteering, so there was no financial cost. I was provided a daily update on their progress. After two and a half days, I received a call at around 4:00 p.m. on a Thursday from accounting, stating they had found batching errors which added up to around $32,000. This was over a month and half period. I called you and told you the news and said it would take about a week before we would start seeing these monies and then deal with people receiving late postings on there credit or debit cards.

I told accounting I would be down Saturday to check the reports. I told the commodore of this meeting and he insisted to be there. I said I would handle it. He then called accounting and said he would be there for the meeting. This made the accounting person very upset and stated she was about to walk if he continued bothering her. I told her to sit and stay and that I would handle this. I wanted to finish up with the horses before engaging in a conversation with the commodore. He ended up calling me before I was done. I just basically said, "If you're not going to listen to me, then do not call me." I hung up the phone. I met the accounting person off site so not to be disturbed. She provided me with a printout of her findings, and I was satisfied with the results. I spent Sunday working on the e-mail sent out to the membership explaining what had happened.

Now we have a special meeting called on what is being dealt with. Even the directors were not buying this.

One week later, there was a matter that took place and started a domino effect. I received a call from the commodore about getting my ladies in order. Once I looked into that, it appeared there was more to the story than my ladies. Having knowledge of a few other incidents, I just got upset and went looking for a way to stop the madness. I did not sign up for this; I left the playground a long time ago.

The commodore, rear commodore, a director, and I attended a YRUSC Seminar at Del Rey Yacht Club in December before engaging our newly elected positions. We received a rather in-depth view of what it is to be expected being on the board and received a booklet of orientation as a member of a board. After reviewing that booklet for a second time, I reviewed our bylaws and found a way to at least call the commodore on his actions.

I had a mentor when I joined this club in 2010. He made a lot of sense to me. He said to me when looking into the club from the balcony, "You don't need to be friends with all these people. You just need to earn their respect." I never forgot that. Before my mentor passed away from cancer, he told me I should get more involved with the club, that I had a lot to offer. I said, "Are you crazy?" I just wanted a good drink and to get out of the weather once in a while. So here I am, all because he asked me to.

Respectfully submitted.

The next morning, I decided to send the commodore another e-mail as well. I also cc'd the board just to let them know I had not let this go.

Good morning,

Good meeting last night! One might think that if you had succeeded installing your choice of a new board member, it might have been different, with the way your agenda read. We did accomplish a lot though. Unfortunately, not all was done. There two more items that should have been presented. You adjourned the meeting improperly. The secretary looked up and said, "Is it over?" A director had to call for proper adjournment. I could have called the meeting back to order, but it was a good meeting and did not want to change the tone.

With that being said, I want to state for the record, even though it is not valid, the items not addressed. The situation with the Coast Guard dinner needs closure. I was to present the total cost for the Coast Guard Dinner in December. Enclosed is a breakdown for the dinner showing we had made a net of $250. In the past, we have always done the dinner at cost. Also the cost of the servers should not have happened. We use volunteers for that so not to raise the cost. Our member who is in the Coast Guard Auxiliary put up the difference so the dinner would happen. It was my understanding that we would total the dinner and cover our cost so any profit would be returned to him in good faith. We had sixty-one people who would not normally have been there on a Saturday night The tally from the bar should reflect a profit from that activity. The Coast Guard is one the Community Services we perform under our nonprofit status. This is an example why we as a board have to establish all business affairs at the November BOD meeting through the January COW because there is no meeting to monitor these events during this period of time.

These decisions are not to be made by few individuals but by the Board. This is now bringing closure to the closed session on February 18. You obviously did not take the time to answer our request for an explanation of your actions. With that being said, I did, and just want it to be stated for the record so we can let that go to rest. I have written an explanation for my actions. We can not sweep these things under the carpet. We are to be held responsible for our actions and behave accordingly. You asked for our help, and I am handing it to you in good faith.

Respect does not come with a title. One must earn it by their actions. As of last night, you're on a roll, so let's keep it rolling forward.

If you're going to continue recording our meetings, that would be the secretary's job and the recordings in her charge. It was stated the recordings were for her benefit. Even though she did not request this, you did. You also need to tell the membership when you are recording the general meetings.

Let's have a good meeting on Friday—it is time to *wow* the masses. Best regards.

I did succeed getting a $250 refund for that gentleman at the April board of directors meeting.

CHAPTER 7

I T WAS THE EVENING OF our March general meeting. All was going well. With the recent issues in our accounting system, there were questions coming from the membership. I was becoming more aware, when there was discontent from the membership, it was usually coming from one source. At this meeting, it was brought up that an audit be done. It was decided to be an in-house audit. There were issues about who would be on the committee, but it was finally decided and voted on. It was obvious that a certain group of individuals were implementing this. I believe it was a good idea. As the vice commodore, it was in my best interest even though the audit was 2013, the year the now commodore was the vice commodore.

As commodore, he involved himself in this audit directing certain areas be looked into. It seemed as sort of a witch hunt. The committee was aware of this intent, but he was the commodore. At least this kept him busy and there were no more incidents at this time.

We were preparing for our opening ceremonies, so our plates were plenty full of things to do. Our opening day was in April, and sometimes there was a conflict with Easter Sunday. Opening days of the various clubs are different times in the spring. Yacht clubs in the same area coordinate the date so they can be easily attended. The bridge members of each club tried to attend as many of the other yacht clubs as possible. This is a traditional and an annual event. There was so much to do to prepare. In our case, we had a specific group that handled the inside of the club for decorations usually in honor of that year's commodore. After the theme is chosen, there is a menu developed that needs preparation—also a sound system, music, refreshments, and a tight program to follow. It is normally the outgoing commodore who is in charge. It is our introduction to the opening of our yachting season with a celebration with those who share the tradition.

The next few months seemed to fly by. The audit was in full motion. This distracted the accounting from being handled because of the load of information needed. There was only one person who knew how to access the membership and financial system. This also distracted the commodore from disturbing anything else.

It became apparent the audit committee was finding problems as they dived deeper into that year. There was nothing bad, just a lot of inconsistencies. The membership roster was not currently updated. There certainly needed to have some procedure protocols be put in place.

I received a call from the commodore in late June stating he wanted to ask the accounting person to train someone new for the accounting position and then resign. The present accounting person was a current member of the club and was to fill the position temporarily until she could be replaced. Our former employee of seven years had to be replaced due to health issues. Our member assuming the position felt she could hold that space in the interim. She had been the treasurer for a few years. The replacement of the accounting person got sidetracked due to many things. I agreed that it was time to address this issue. I stated I would support this action.

He called me a few days later and stated he was taking this member out for lunch. He would be introducing that process to her. I received a call from the accounting person stating that the commodore had invited her for lunch and asked if I knew what it was about. I did not feel I was to interfere with the process since I was not able to be present. This was not the first time the commodore had taken this person to lunch. The commodore and his wife had taken lunches previously with this person. It must have been his mannerism that made her call me. The commodore did invite another member to lunch. His wife was not present. This member was the audit committee person who had not been working in the office but was doing the audit.

The conversation started, and then he just said, "I would like you to think of resigning." We all knew this was a temporary position and it was time to train someone as an employee. It was stated in the bylaws that a member cannot hold an employee paid position. This interim position was approved by the board the year before at the last board of directors meeting in November because of its urgency. Well, the conversation started going south after a few more words. He then asked for her keys. I was told they returned to the yacht club. She called me and stated in a few words what had happened and said she needed to make a bank deposit and she had been relieved of her duties as the accounting person. I told her to make the deposits and I would be down later because I was scheduled to cook the Wednesday evening meal. I then received a call from the commodore that the accounting person had left the building with all the money and he was calling the police. I told him I had heard from that person and she said she was making the deposit and I would be down at 4:00 p.m. He said he would give me until 6:00 p.m.

I arrived at the club to find a locksmith changing the lock to the office. I did hear from the accounting person who stated she had forgotten to photocopy checks for our records. I suggested Kinko's. She said she would meet me in the club parking lot at 5:30 p.m. and had no intention of entering the yacht club. For me, this was very disturbing. This person had been a member of this yacht club for more than twenty years as well as serving as a commodore. She was commodore when I joined in 2010.

The commodore and his wife arrived for dinner. I assured him there was no need to involve the police. I had made contact with her and I would have the bank receipts and anything else she had in her possession. This member called from the parking lot, and I retrieved all items. I told the commodore where the box was containing these articles because I did not have a new key.

This happened on Wednesday, June 30. It was before the Fourth of July weekend. I already had company coming into town for the holiday weekend. I told the commodore, "You created this, you can handle all affairs until next week." He called for a special meeting to address this issue the following week.

We all arrived for the special meeting. He stated what had happened in his words. Some directors were aware and some were not. He said he had informed me of his intent to ask the member to step down from this position. He then stated that I told him I support his actions. I raised my hand and got the floor. I said, "Yes, I agreed it was time to set this right, and I have your back, but not the shit storm you have created. This is not how to conduct business." He stated she got very upset when I approached the subject. I said, "Maybe it was the way you presented it. We had already been discussing the best way to replace her position. You know that you and this member are like oil and water. Then you said you were going to call the police! The words we were looking for are *finesse* and *respect*. Obviously these words are not in your vocabulary. I believe the board should at least offer a written apology for his action." It was unanimously accepted.

Unfortunately, that did not happen. A flurry of e-mail among the board started exchanging, resulting in a change of heart. When the rear commodore put out his version, I immediately said I would not sign it. The majority of the board continued to push for an apology. Finally I wrote one and sent it to the board members with no resolve. I ended up just sending a copy to that member and apologized for apologizing. She understood the craziness. She had served on the board and was commodore and was aware of the contempt some people had for others.

I called her daily, and she would at least pick up or return my calls. I was very concerned how she was doing. She had put her heart and soul into this club after losing her husband. She was only doing the best she could. Now she was being shamed and blamed for this. This was not right.

One saving grace was there had been a club bus trip to Laughlin, Nevada, for golfing and gambling in May. She was one of many members who attended. Once they returned, you could tell something special had happened. She and one of our members had become very close.

Fortunately, that relationship blossomed, which helped with the devastating blow of this encounter with the commodore. That relationship flourished until her recent death this year.

During the special meeting about the accounting upset, it was approved to hire a temp from a temp agency. The commodore had already made contact and was setting up interviews. He and the audit person were prescreening applicants. I was called to set in on the person that seemed most qualified by them.

I came down the next afternoon to assist in the interview as vice commodore. Her resume looked good. I was not sure of her personal capabilities. They seemed a bit scattered and not focused for an accounting person. After dismissing her from the interview, we had a discussion, and it was noted that was probably due to nervousness from the interview. I agreed with them. Maybe that might just be it. This hiring of this person would now be up to the board.

Our July BOD meeting was on the following Tuesday. The hiring of this person was discussed and approved at that meeting. The other highlight was who was going to train the person since no one knew the system. Our accounting program was QuickBooks. I was familiar with the program but not in the matter of this yacht club. I had already spoken to our member who had been doing the books until being relieved of that position. I asked if there was any way she would be willing to help me make this transition easier than it was going to be. She agreed to help on one stipulation. I had to be present at all times when she would be working with the new person and no commodore present. When I approached the board with this proposal, the commodore went ballistic, no way. I said, "This is not your call. You made this mess and I have to clean it up." After some heated discussion, a motion was made and a vote was taken giving me the authority to do what was necessary to get back on track.

I called the temp agency, requesting their person to meet on Thursday along with our past accounting person and give her an introduction to our system. I also asked the accounting member to make up a list of all that needed doing and when it was to be done. A working schedule of things to do and the passwords, safe combinations necessary to run the office. There was nothing on record or if there was it was not current.

We met that Thursday and reviewed our current system. The temp was taking notes. She did have an understanding of QuickBooks as her resume implied. We focused on what was to be done immediately and checks that needed to be issued. We were already two weeks behind. The day went pretty well. A decision was made by all that we would return on Monday and see what could be accomplished by the end of that week. I thanked both of them for their efforts.

We accomplished a lot once focused on the issues. I reported to the board via e-mail on our progress Thursday and said we would be back in the office on Monday. I would be reporting back on Friday with an update.

The next week came, and we started moving forward. The temp's nervousness became more apparent. She was not listening to what was being explained but overreacting to the explanation. Her notes were not very thorough even for her own interpretation. It was becoming a bit of a challenge. I said, "Just listen to what this person is trying to say and look at what she is referring to." A light went on, and we were back on track.

This process was starting to wear on me. I was driving an hour and a half, arriving at 10:00 a.m., overseeing this transition and babysitting at the same time. Yes, we were making progress, but it was going to take more time. I left at 3:00 p.m. to return home to do my own business.

CHAPTER 8

On that Friday, my girlfriend, Sally, had a doctor's appointment. They were to discuss her progress with her cancer. That news was not good, and she was to start chemotherapy the next week. The cancer was back and spreading quickly. Surgery was out of the question.

Sally was now realizing the reality before her. She had already put her personal business in order after the last scare. We talked about her feelings of doing chemotherapy again. She did not want to but did make the decision to try.

I wanted to be there for her as much she would let me. She was trying to run me off, but I refused to walk. She was a very strong person and had the personality to go with it. I said, "You had just better get used to it. I am going nowhere." I was not allowed to take her to her chemotherapy sessions, but that did not stop me from showing up and holding her hand and talking a little until she would ask me to leave. She still had me over for dinners she prepared, and we watched old movies on the couch.

She had gotten herself a beautiful Aussie puppy she named Stetson. After this last notice of the cancer returning, she decided she was not up for the task and had to let her beloved dog go. I was never told where he went. I assumed to her ex-husband, who had the same breed.

It was a long weekend of contemplation. I decided to contact the board and let them know I just could not continue this driving and overseeing this transition. I recommended that the audit person be the one to oversee this since she lived in the area and was working on the audit of our financials. When I did not receive any comment on this proposal, I decided it was best I stepped down as vice commodore but I would remain on the board as a director so not to disturb the order. I had some personal issues that needed to be attended to.

This got immediate attention from the board. They did not respond to the proposal but were very sympathetic to my situation to stepping down as the vice commodore. I had written this in my article in our in-house monthly publication to the membership for the August addition. I gave my usual updates and thanked those who made our events successful from the previous month. I stated, "I regretfully step down from vice commodore due to the changes in the accounting area. A need was imminent, but the manner of change has created a situation that needs full attention to make it successful. I spent a week commuting to help make this change go forward. The time needed is more than I can do, considering my business, responsibilities, distance, and cost of the commute. I have to pass the torch to someone who can implement our commodore's wishes. It was my pleasure serving you. Thank you. Smooth sailing and happy trails."

When this news was released to the membership, I received calls and e-mail on this subject. One suggestion after hearing what my personal issues were was to remain as vice commodore and ask for a leave of absence. "If you have not made the resignation and the board has not ratified, then ask to be reinstated. I am sure they would be much happier with that solution."

I spoke to Sally. She said she could agree with that, with all I had been doing up to this time. I put an e-mail out to the board asking to be reinstated but taking a leave of absence of sixty days starting the day I first announced my decision on July 23 and I would return to duty September 23. The majority of the board was positive about my decision, but the commodore and the rear commodore were not supportive. The commodore was not going to let me assume the vice commodore role. I just stated it would be discussed at the next board of directors meeting.

The commodore decided that he was calling a special meeting of the general membership to discuss this. The special notice was sent out to the members, which had to be a two-week notice prior to the meeting by mail. It was scheduled to be held before the general meeting that August. The commodore had been told this was a decision for the board, not the membership. They had chosen me for the position originally.

During this time, I was not serving as the vice commodore. It was stated in the bylaws that the rear commodore would assume the position of the vice commodore. He/she will hold that office until the return, resignation, removal, or death of that person.

I assumed that the rear commodore had taken the seat, but actually this gave the commodore the opportunity to control the accounting office with no contest from the rear commodore now acting as the vice commodore.

The August board meeting was now in session. The decision on whether or not to accept my return was now on the agenda. A motion was made to accept my return. The commodore gave his reasons why this could not happen. Now it was my turn to address the board. I gave all the facts of this matter. After answering a few questions, it was now time to vote. It was unanimously accepted that I be reinstated as vice commodore but would be on a sixty-day leave of absence, returning September 23. The rear commodore would continue doing the vice commodore's duties until my return on the twenty-third of September.

The next day, I had an e-mail sent out to the membership stating the facts of this matter, and the special meeting was now cancelled. There would only be the general meeting on Friday night at 7:00 p.m. "Please be there, this is the evening we announce the nominees running for the 2015 board of directors."

I had never been contacted by any member of the nominating committee. If I was to continue and run for commodore, I would have to be voted on to the 2015 board of directors. A person can be nominated from the floor by another member. Since I was on a leave of absence, I was not required to sit with the board at the general meeting. I would have to be present if I were nominated from the floor to accept the nomination.

The general meeting was called to session. An item to be presented to the membership was about the audit by a committee member. It was stated that they were far from done and would need at least two more months. When explaining in further detail about their findings, there was an outburst from the commodore's wife. She stated that when serving as vice commodore, I had presigned checks that were in an unsecured area in the office. One past commodore interrupted her and said, "Why are you saying anything?" She repeated herself. Another member reiterated again, "What is your point?" Once again she said my name. At this time the audit person who was giving the update asked her to sit down. We have found no theft or wrongdoing. What we did find were some procedural problems that would be addressed in the near future.

I was not interested in defending myself. I knew exactly why I had presigned those five checks. They had been used before the audit, and there were receipts to support these expenses. We were on cash only on delivery with a few of our vendors. Not because we were not paying our invoices. It was their posting to our account in a timely manner. That finally got straightened out. I also lived an hour and a half away. There was not always someone to sign those checks because we would not know the amount until the time of the delivery. I was furious about her outburst. She had certainly embarrassed herself more than me in front of the membership.

It was now time to announce the nominees by the nominating committee. There were four candidates. Now the commodore addressed the membership asking if there were any nominations from the floor. A past commodore raised his hand and said yes. He nominated me. When I was asked if I would accept, I stood and said yes. This was the only nomination from the floor. That part was now closed. The commodore said to the nominees, "You will each have a few minutes to address the membership on why you want to be a member of the board and a little about yourself. Please be brief so I do not have to cut you short."

Well, the new nominees looked at me and said, "You should go first since you're on the board." I said, "You all go first. I have something more to address. You decide who will go first, and I will be the last to speak." Each nominee addressed the membership.

It was now my turn. I introduced myself as "your comeback vice commodore. I am currently on a leave of absence and will be returning to my duties on September 23, as was stated to all of you in my e-mail." I then explained the presigned checks that the commodore's wife was accusing me of doing. I said, "When you say my name once, twice, and then a third time, enough is enough—there is a new sheriff in town. I am running for the 2015 board and would appreciate your vote. Thank you." I walked out of the room and into the bar. Several people joined me. The commodore then said the meeting was not over, but that did not stop people leaving the room. The business they came to hear had just been heard.

Several people came up and said, "We have no question of your honesty" and "You have my support." That was rude and uncalled for. After the meeting, the commodore's wife came up to me and said she had not meant it that way. But she did not apologize for the outburst. I did not give her the time of day. I just went about my conversations with others and then retired for the evening. The person giving the audit update approached me, asking if I was mad at her. I said, "Absolutely not." She asked if she could have a word with me. I said, "Yes, but let's go outside." She proceeded to tell me about working in the office and she had questions. I said I was not the acting vice commodore now and would not be returning until the end of my leave of absence and then explained Sally's situation. She was unaware of Sally's condition. She wished us both the best, and we parted company.

I shared the story with Sally. She was pretty mad but was not surprised by this action. She asked, "Are you really serious about running again with those people acting like that?" I was still pondering the idea but was not going to let those people belittle me. She said, "I will support whatever you want to do. There is not much you can do for me. I am dying, and that is not going to change. It is only a matter of time. You do what is right for you."

My local close friends, who had known me for over twenty years, asked, "What is up at your yacht club?" I had shared some of the issues I was encountering. Their question was, "Why are you doing this? It seems those people are ungrateful to have you solving their problem. It sounds more like they thrive on chaos." I explained to them who were mostly ten years younger that I was having a senior moment. Now at sixty-five years of age and avoiding these kinds of people most of my adult life, it was time to stand my ground. I felt like someone had to step up and show them how it worked, following proper protocol and abiding by the bylaws as written. No ego involved, just a matter of fact. Being commodore was not on my bucket list. There came a time to draw the line in the sand and move forward not looking back at the naysayers. Action speaks louder than words. That can be for good or bad. Fortunately I am not a terrorist. More like a terror to the old guard protecting their interest.

I remember sitting in the bar with the treasurer and her husband. There was a celebration of life for a member in the main dining room. I was now the commodore. There was a very large turnout for this gentleman. It was now time to refresh their drinks before continuing to share stories of their adventures over many years. As the crowd was entering the bar, I overheard a gentleman ask a past commodore if the old guard was still running the show. The past commodore saw me before he answered. He looked back at the past member and said no. "We are under new management."

CHAPTER 9

I T WAS NOW LATE AUGUST and I was thinking I should check in with the audit member who has been working in the office. I wanted to get on board with activities so as not to walk into a mess.

I e-mailed her about the bar manager and the commodore's upcoming meeting. I was sure it was soon but not sure when. The bar manager and the commodore did not mix well. She did reply and said it would be that afternoon. I called the bar manager, who did not pick up and left a message saying, "I would like to know how your meeting goes. I will be returning soon and if there is a problem, please let me know." Later he responded, "Thanks, I have this covered."

I received a reply from the audit person. Her question was who was in charge. A little baffled by this question with no further information, I replied by stating the vice commodore was and explained his duties.

There was a bonding meeting of the men's cooking group that evening, and I was bringing the meat. It was a good meeting and meal. The person who had been the leader for 2014 had announced his choice for his replacement. This was accepted by the group. We also discussed the dinners remaining on the calendar until the end of the year. All bases were now covered.

After returning home, I had received another reply from the audit person on my explanation of the person in charge, the vice commodore. Her reply read, "If the vice commodore is the one in charge, he had better grab the proverbial bull by the horns. Things are out of control. If you want to know more, call me!"

I did the next day, and I got an earful. I was not surprised at all by what she was saying. I had suspected as much but had no knowledge of what was happening. I was on a leave of absence helping Sally with support on her situation, which was most important. I did not want to be disturbed with this. After the audit person unloaded on me, we talked about a possible solution. She was saying she was now working in the office with the temp. There was a lot to be done, but no one was doing much about it. She said, "I do not know what I should be doing at this point. I feel I am overstepping my bounds." She stated that the temp was working less hours and was not doing any bookwork on previous financials before her hiring of July 14. The commodore was in the office constantly talking with the temp and giving direction. She also stated she had not seen the rear commodore, now acting as vice commodore, in the office.

I told her we had not had financials for the board or general meetings at all this year. There was a board of directors meeting coming up on September 16 and a general meeting the week after on Friday. We needed to get our books in order. "I do not care how many hours she works, but that is the focus I want you to present to her." It was now August 27. This was the Labor Day weekend coming up. Monday was the holiday. She said that she and her husband were invited to the cruise up to Santa Barbara and would be having brunch at the Santa Barbara Yacht Club. I told her I would join all of them there. "In the meantime, I will announce my return on Monday, the first of September, via e-mail to the board and then to the membership. Let's keep this between us until that time. You can inform the commodore of your plan of attack to get our financials in order. With my return, you will be working under me. He does not have to know."

I met our members at Santa Barbara Yacht Club, and we had a great brunch. I just looked at my audit person and smiled. No one asked anything about my returning. They all wanted to know how Sally was doing.

The commodore was not happy about my returning early. He stated in his e-mail that I needed to check with him and the acting vice commodore before doing anything in the office. He said many changes had happened and I needed to be brought up to speed. I replied, "What changes? I have gotten all the e-mail the other board members have. I have seen nothing about any changes." And then other board members started chiming in on what changes. The treasurer said she was unaware of any changes. The board was unaware of these changes and would all like to hear about them. Our next board meeting was on Tuesday, the sixteenth. There was no urgent need for a special meeting. I already had my bases covered. Let these two bridge members address the board at that time. No more was said on that subject.

On September 3, the commodore announced he had a meeting with the audit committee person who was helping in the office. She had prepared a list of things that she and our temp person would be working on in order to get financials for our upcoming board meeting and the general meeting. He was quite proud of his announcement.

I would speak to the audit person daily if not every other day. I left them alone in the office. My presence was unnecessary, and I did not want to disturb that situation. They stayed on schedule and had current financials for both meetings.

CHAPTER 10

I T WAS TIME FOR OUR board of directors meeting. I noticed that the commodore had the hiring of the temp person on the agenda. I called the audit person and informed her of his plan. She was to attend our meeting that night and make her presentation. I asked her to have the temp come to the meeting. Some board members had not met this person. I only thought it was right to do so. I failed to inform anyone of her invitation.

Another item on his agenda was the introduction of an interim director to replace one who had suffered a heart attack. He had been hospitalized for the past week. I called his daughter the day of our meeting to get an update. She said he seemed pretty good but needed a lot of rest and should be released in a few more days. She mentioned nothing of stepping down as a director. I thanked her for the update and said I would be reporting this to the board. It looked like the commodore was up to his usual antics. He had named the same person as interim director he had tried when the same thing happened earlier in the year in his agenda.

When the commodore announced his choice for the interim director, he gave this person the opportunity to address the board. He started out saying he would consider this but was concerned about some wrongdoing he did not want to be responsible for. This was only rumored, but he would be hesitant to be on the board. He would want to sign an agreement stating his non-responsibility in case any action should take place. He was asked, "What are you referring to?" He said it was a rumor and would say no more. At this point, it was time to confront the commodore. "Why are we listening to this person? Do you have a written and signed resignation from that director?" "Well, no, but I went to see him with his son in-law and daughter Susie."

"No, her name is Cindy," was the correction by a director.

Well anyway, he said he wanted this person to take his place on the board. It then was stated by a director, without a written signed resignation by this director, there would be no further conversation. The individual awaiting confirmation walked out of the room without further comment.

The audit person gave her presentation updating the board on her and the temp's progress. I thanked her for all her hard work. She looked at me and said, "Should I?" I said yes. She informed the temp the board was now ready for her entrance. The commodore's jaw dropped and then asked, "What are you doing here?" She said that the audit person had asked her to come so she could address the board about possible employment as our employee. I introduced her. She spoke for a few moments about liking working at our club. She answered a few questions. The commodore was trying to get her to leave, which she did momentarily.

We continued our usual business after that. It was getting a little late. The commodore was calling for a closed session to talk about the hiring of this temp person. It was stated the only people who were here were board members. All others had left earlier. We continued in an open meeting. The commodore continued recording this meeting.

The commodore started his conversation saying the temp person had resigned from the temp agency about three weeks ago. She would like to work for us at a rate of twelve dollars an hour. She did not want to make a lot of money. "I would like to hire her at that rate until the end of my year."

His statement opened the floodgates for questions. It was September 16, and she had quit her job with the agency three weeks ago. So who was paying her now? He said the agency. How could that be if she was not on their payroll, which was at twenty-eight dollars an hour? This Q&A went on for over thirty-three minutes. Yes, that was way too long, but he was recording it. I thought, *Just let it go until you can't take any longer.* It was getting way off track. I finally decided this had to stop. I made a motion to continue with the agency for thirty days. After a short comment session, a vote was called. It was unanimously accepted to continue with the agency. I said I would make the phone call and talked with the person who handled our contract. I would be reporting back to the board members after I got to the bottom of this tomorrow via e-mail. They were satisfied, and the meeting was adjourned.

Wednesday morning, I called the agency's office and asked to speak with the person who was handling our account. When she answered the phone, I introduced myself. She asked, "How can I help you?" I said, "We had our board of directors meeting last night. We made the decision to stay with your agency for thirty more days." She said that our contract had been closed and the woman working told her she was quitting because of lack of hours. She was not working enough to stay on. That was late August. She then asked me if she was working for us. I stated yes.

She said, "I will call her and get her hours and start you back up again." I was perplexed by her answer. "So you are going to call her and we'll just move forward?" "Yes" was her answer. Mine was, "OK. Let me know if there is any problem." I thanked her and sat down and typed up an e-mail to the board on my findings. We had signed a contract with this agency to the effect if we hired this person within a certain time frame, we would have to buy out the contract at a percentage. I sent out the e-mail. The responses were favorable, but it seemed too easy. One of the directors asked if he could inquire about her quitting. The person I spoke to was out of the office that Friday. He spoke to the receptionist. She had a slightly different story. After informing me of this, I called again to speak with my connection. I was told she was out for a long weekend and would be back on Monday. I said, "Fine, it is not that important." Thirty minutes later, the person from the agency was calling from Arizona where she was visiting. I just asked if what she said that the temp quit herself was right. "The commodore had nothing to do with it?" She said he had called and they had talked about a buyout. She said she had never encountered a person who could not understand their buyout policy. She stated she talked herself blue in the face before just giving up on any further explanation. I said, "So we are all good to go?" She said yes. I apologized for interrupting her holiday and thanked her for her time. We would not be bothering her anymore.

The following day was Saturday. I happened to be down at the club. The temp was in the office working. I called a director who lived on his boat asking him to meet me at the yacht club. I wanted to ask the temp her side of the story. He agreed and came over. There was an event that members were decorating upstairs for. Among those members was the commodore's wife.

I had made a decision with my current situation that anything dealing with the office would have to be witnessed by another member of the board. This was why I contacted the director. We entered the office and said hi to the temp person. We entered into the office through the door which connected to the club. The other door led outside to the sidewalk and marina. I locked the door we came in so as not to be disturbed. The other door was left open. The director asked, "When did you quit the agency? Did someone offer you a job here?" Her answer was not very clear. She tried changing the subject when in came the commodore. He had a computer keyboard. He said she had told him hers was not working very well. The director reached out and took the keyboard and said he would switch them out. Well, the receptacle on the computer was not compatible.

We figured his wife had called him and informed him we were in the office talking to the temp. At that point, I had no further questions. It seemed we already had our answer. The director and I thought her keyboard was fine. We had been in the office and on the computer the night before. After that, my communication with the temp was kept very limited. I had my audit person who could get me any information necessary without alarming anyone. I was waiting it out until the next board meeting in October.

It was now the day of the general meeting in September when the new board was elected. I received a call from the treasurer. She asked how things were going. How was Sally doing? I said things were good. Sally was doing the best to cope with her situation. The chemotherapy was not helping. She was looking to get other opinions. The treasurer said, "I want to let you know we have decided to postpone our leaving to cruise Mexico and beyond until next fall. Just wanted to say if you would like, I will remain treasurer for your year."

I did not hesitate and said yes. "That is great news and thank you for your support." I asked if she had a moment to talk.

She said, "Yes, what's up?"

I said I had reservations about running for commodore. There was a lot going in my life. Sally was dying, and some friends had just lost their business to a shady partnership agreement, and another friend had just lost his right hand due to an accident at his winery. Thinking about them versus that yacht club, they seemed more important. She said, "I fully understand what you are saying, but you are the one who can get this club back on track. Run for the board, run for commodore next month, and carry us in to the New Year. Then do whatever you need to do. You have a lot of support from the membership." I told her I had already spoken to Sally about taking the position. She totally supported the idea as long as it was what I wanted to do. I then told the treasurer I would run for the board. I needed to make a strong presentation to the membership to let them know how I felt if they wanted me back on the board. She said, "That is great news. I will see you tonight."

I hung up the phone and began thinking of my presentation. It was going to be very important to make my case for running for the board, including my intent to be the next commodore. It was equally important that they know I was not there to waste my time and get caught in the usual crap that seemed to surface at meetings.

I had a briefcase I had never used. I chose three items that fit in this briefcase. These were tools used in my trade. I placed a few other items in the case I thought pertinent to this introduction. It was all coming together. I was feeling confident about my decision and my approach to the membership seeking their vote to continue on the board, ultimately becoming their commodore.

The parking lot was quite full as I pulled up to the club. It was just ten minutes until the meeting would be called to order. I did not want to spend much time talking to anyone. I just wanted to get the show on the road. The energy level seemed elevated. Someone said to me, "I thought you were going to ride a white horse up the stairs." I answered no; I had just brought a briefcase. It was a full house. I had called members reminding them to attend, and an e-mail had been put out to the membership stating the importance of their presence, if they were interested in the future of our club.

The meeting was called to order. It was announced that we had a quorum. We did the Pledge of Allegiance to the flag, an invocation by our chaplain, and got down to business. It was now time to present the nominees for the board to the membership. After they were announced, each had a few moments to address the membership before the voting of the four positions available. There were five candidates running. I said I would go last. Each candidate spoke and pleaded their case for running for the board. It was now my time. I was at the podium since I was on the board. I introduced myself as the comeback vice commodore. I picked up my briefcase and said, "I would like to show you a few tools of my trade." I unlatched my briefcase, reaching into it and pulling out a clear bag. I said, "These are predator flies. We put them down on the ground so we get rid of the flies bothering us." I set them down and pulled out a bull-whip. "We do not hit the horses with this, we use it to produce the sound that gets their attention and which straightens them out." My third and final item was an emasculator. "We use this to rid anything hanging in the way." I had their complete attention now. I then said, "I'm running for the board for one reason and that is to be your commodore." I said thank you and sat down. This caused quite a stir in a positive way. The commodore took the podium and asked if there were any question for the candidates. A member raised her hand who happened to be my audit person from the office.

She was asked, "What is your question?"

She said, "What is your vision for us?"

I thanked her for her question and said, "Now that I have your attention." I pulled the three manuals out of my briefcase. I picked up the gavel and hit the podium and said, "I will use this to get your attention and use these three booklets to govern this club. This one is a copy of your bylaws, this is a copy of Robert's Rules of Order to run meetings." I held up the last manual and said, "This is a booklet on how to run a yacht club. In this booklet, there is a 'dos and don'ts' list for directors and officers. When you use the 'don'ts' list as your 'do' list and the 'do' list as your 'don'ts,' it does not work that way. This is my vision for you." There were no more questions. Ballots had already been passed out, so members were told only one ballot per member and to write four different names only for the four seats open for the board. The ballots were collected, and a fifteen-minute recess was called. I just remained sitting in my seat as people headed to the bar or just started moving about.

The meeting was called back to order. The meeting continued as scheduled. If they called out the results of the election before the end, most people would probably leave the room. It was now time to announce the new board members. They were called out in alphabetical order. The first, then the second, now the third, and the fourth was announced, which was me. The first hurdle was now cleared. The meeting was adjourned.

Many members came over and shook my hand. They were pretty blown away by my approach for running for commodore. It was quite the topic in the bar. I stayed around for a short while. I wanted to see Sally. I called her and shared the news. She was happy for me.

Chapter 11

WELL, IT DID NOT TAKE long to start receiving e-mails from the commodore and rear commodore about my presentation Friday night. I was being asked to apologize for my ranting, as they put it. They said they were receiving complaints about my comments. I just laughed and knew where these complaints were coming from. I replied, "How many complaints have you received?" I had no intention of apologizing until after the elections in October. We would see then how many people took offense to my honesty. I only shared what I was feeling. There were no more exchanges on that subject.

Rumors started surfacing on who would want a commodore who was a quitter. This was in reference to my taking a leave of absence earlier in the year. Next was a group was trying to rally support for the rear commodore to run against me for commodore. I again took no thought to these subjects that were drifting around the club. I said what I said to cut through this bullshit.

Now I was thinking it was time to have some fun. I found no reason to campaign for commodore. But I did have an idea. When I was serving as the leader of the men's cooking group, I was bestowed the name of El Ranchero. During that year, each lead chef from each meal cooked would receive a medal with my picture on front and the dinner they had cooked on the back.

These medals were attached to a ribbon so they could be worn around the neck. This was a tradition within this cooking group. The person who started this was known as El Hefe. He had these made up each year. He had taken a picture of me with my cowboy hat on and incorporated a hat band with my year. I took one of these medals and had campaign buttons made with that picture and had the date changed on the hat band to match my year running for commodore.

When these buttons started surfacing, they created quite a buzz. A few people were not happy about this, but they spread so fast it would look ridiculous if you were going to make a scene about it. I was not passing them out. I only had them made. The comment made by the rear commodore's wife was somebody really wanted that position. It was great. The gentleman referred to as El Hefe went up to the club photographer and questioned her, "Did you have anything to do with this?" She claimed, "No." It just got funnier as the elections were getting closer.

We had members from the yacht club staying at the ranch after the election. I had given a weekend at the ranch to be raffled off at one of our events at the club. This was the group who bought the weekend. They were all going to the Hitching Post II in Buellton for dinner.

Knowing this and because I knew most of the staff, I took a handful of the campaign buttons to them. I let them know these people were coming and to wear the pins. If asked, "Do you know this guy?" they were to say, "Yes, he is running for mayor." The members got a kick out of that. "We thought he was just running for commodore of our yacht club."

I had spoken to the audit committee person. She informed me she was going on the trip to Fuji with many other members in the beginning of October and would be gone ten days. She also informed me that the membership invoices were being held up from mailing until she returned so all member data could be reviewed and corrected. I wished her a fun trip and safe return. I would assist when she returned.

What ended up happening was the commodore gave all member addresses to the temp and had her load all that information into our accounting system. She then made invoices and sent them out the day the members flew out for Fuji. This created quite a mess. That information was not cleared before sending, and a lot of people were very upset. After seeing this, I had an e-mail sent to the membership apologizing for this error. "Please ignore those invoices that some of the audit committee had left town for that trip, and we will be going over all of this information to get corrected before sending any further invoices out. Thank you for your patience." I thought to myself, *That SOB.*

I waited until the return of the audit committee before reacting to how I really felt. They called for a meeting and I said I would be there. When I walked in, the commodore was talking with the committee. He was being asked, "Why did you have those invoices sent out before clearing it with us first?"

He said, "We are owed a lot of money. I am going to get it."

I asked him, "What are you doing here?"

He said it was his meeting.

I said, "No, it is not. If you want to stay, sit down and shut up. You created this mess, and this has to be straightened out immediately." After a few more words, we moved on getting things in order.

It was now time for our board of directors meeting for October. The new board members were invited if they wished to see how our business was being conducted. The meeting was called to order, and we got things going. A copy of the minutes from the last meeting were being passed out to be read and approved. A copy was provided for the new members. One part read about the director possibly being replaced. That director was now in attendance at this meeting. He had recovered from his heart attack. A new director asked, "Why was he being replaced?" He was sitting right there.

I said, "Read a little further and you will see the outcome."

The director said, "I don't remember much, I was on a morphine drip." We all just laughed and moved on. We did our business as usual. I had asked for a closed session be put on the agenda. I had something to discuss with the board, which had to be said in private. A recess was called for five minutes before the closed session was to start. This gave the new members a moment to visit before having to be dismissed because they were not allowed to sit in a closed session. After the five-minute recess, the meeting was called back to order. We now went into a closed session.

I decided to make a formal complaint against the commodore for his failure to notify the board of his action in continuing working with the temp person after she quit the agency. They were unaware of his action. I further stated that this person was on the property unemployed, uninsured, and was not aware of who was paying her. I found his action inappropriate, which also threatened liability to the yacht club. If any accident had occurred during that time, the yacht club would have been liable, meaning the board was responsible. We were unaware while working in the office from September 1 to September 16, the day of the board meeting, she was basically unemployed after her quitting the agency in late August. We were also in a breach of the contract that was signed by the commodore, stating that her contract had to be bought if she was hired. It also stated that she could not work for us for a certain period if she had quit the agency. I was calling him out on his decision to keep us in the dark. No one had realized that my coming back on September 1 brought this to a head. What if I had waited finishing my leave of absence on September 23? What could have happened then? The audit person stated the temp had not been working very many hours and she was also unaware that the temp had quit the agency. She did know of her desire to be hired by the yacht club.

The commodore seemed confused that this was a problem. He was still trying to get her hired and this time offered the buyout plan. When this subject was proposed, I made a motion that we not hire her and cancel the contract with the agency on Friday, October 31. After a little further discussion, it was put to a vote. I was asked if I had a plan. I said yes, that I had run an ad on Craigslist for this position during a ten-day period. This was when our people went to Fuji. I had eight potential candidates. I had received more resumes, but these were the ones I felt most qualified. I would use the treasurer, the audit person, and myself to interview these people.

CHAPTER 12

UPON FINDING THE RIGHT CANDIDATE, I would ask the board's permission to hire. A vote was taken, and it was the majority of the board that approved this motion. The rear commodore abstained. I had sent him an e-mail asking if he knew about the temp quitting and being hired to continue on in the office after the audit person put out her to-do list. I received no reply to that e-mail but a reply on another matter from a different e-mail. No matter, the commodore was responsible for this, and he now had seven days to respond to this complaint in writing. I called the temp agency the next day to inform them of the board decision to cancel our contract with them and that she would not be hired by the club. They were fine with our decision. I told them we were hiring our own person and thanked them for their service. I was told by the agency spokesperson that she would not be told about her dismissal until 5:00 p.m. on the thirty-first. In our meeting, I stated that if she heard anything about being dismissed before then I would know who to talk to if that happened. I was staring at the commodore when I was saying this.

Toward the end of the seven days, I and another director called for a special meeting. When calling a special meeting, a notice of two days via e-mail is required and an agenda posted on the subject matter. No other subjects were to be discussed. The agenda was to request permission to hire the person we felt most qualified, after having our interviews and whether or not the complaint against the commodore was sustained and warranted action against him.

The secretary sent out the notice of the special meeting being called by two directors as stated in the bylaws. I contacted our parliamentarian to witness the meeting before we would call it into session because of the problems we encountered several months earlier. The commodore, rear commodore, and two directors said they would be unable to make the meeting and we should cancel it. There were five members of the board available for the meeting. We had a quorum, so the meeting was still on.

The evening of the meeting, the parliamentarian approved that our meeting was in order and was excused. The meeting was called to order. After explaining the interview process, a motion was made to hire an accounting employee to fill the position. The vote was unanimous. The next thing was to decide if the commodore was wrong in his action with the previous temp person.

The commodore did not respond to the board's request to submit a written response to the complaint made at the closed session against him. I had asked the secretary to ask the commodore for the recording he made of that meeting. He finally gave her a copy. The recordings were supposed to be for her benefit, but she had none of the recordings in her possession as the secretary. I asked one of the members of the board to take that copy and extract the commodore's conversation explaining to the board of her quitting and his wanting to hire her. This conversation was over thirty-three minutes. I wanted the board members present to hear this conversation again and see if the complaint should be considered sustained. After reviewing the recording a motion was made asking if the complaint against the commodore was sustained. A vote was called, and all in attendance agreed it was sustained. There were five votes in favor, and none abstained. No further action was required until the next board meeting. The meeting was adjourned.

It was now time for the October annual general meeting, which would be the last one for the year. This would be when the bridge officers would be voted in for the next year. The meeting was called to order. The usual program resumed, and it was time for the election of the bridge. The commodore's position was being asked for nominations from the floor. One gentleman, who was a past commodore, raised his hand. He nominated me and gave his reasons. I stood and accepted the nomination. It was now a second request for anyone else. Another gentleman raised his hand and said the rear commodore's name and gave his comments why the rear commodore should be commodore. This gentleman was also a past commodore. He was also the proposed interim director who never got on the board. The rear commodore stood and went to the podium and stated he wished to not run for the commodore position and declined the nomination.

The question was asked, "Are there are any more nominees?" There was none. The floor was now closed and a vote called. It was unanimously accepted that I was now the commodore. After accepting the vote as commodore, I said, "Thank you. I have something I want to say. I want to apologize to anyone who was offended by my presentation at the September meeting. What I had to say was directed at the board, not to the membership. Secondly, I heard a rumor was going around stating I was a quitter. Why would you want a commodore who is a quitter? This was referring to my leave of absence earlier in the year. Sometimes there are more important issues in life that need personal attention. I returned as soon as it seemed right, which was twenty-two days earlier than expected." I was staring at the member who had started that rumor.

The rear commodore accepted his nomination to vice commodore with no challengers. A rear commodore was chosen from the directors with no challengers. After the meeting was adjourned, a round of drinks was customarily bought by the new commodore for the members. That was just fine with me. I called Sally and told her the news. She was happy for me. I brought my good white Stetson for the photo shoot. I thought, *Ye-fucking-hah!* It was time to get this rodeo on.

After I was elected as the incoming commodore, I got a letter from our ladies' cooking group. They were an in-house self-governed group with their own bylaws. This letter was stating that they had an internal problem that I needed to address. The letter explained what happened when voting the people in charge for the next year. A member of theirs had been accepted to a position by the majority of their members, but the women writing this complaint did not think she should serve in that position. Our bylaws stated a ram member of the yacht club could not hold a position on our board unless they were a full member. Their bylaws did not cover this situation. So now they wanted the board to make the decision for them by using the club's bylaws. Not our problem, especially when their majority saw no issue with this.

A ram member of the yacht club is a racing member who pays less to join because they represent the club in racing events at their own expense. It is stated in the bylaws as a ram member, you do not have a vote but can fly the burgee and participate in all other activities. Unfortunately, some regular members view these members as second-class citizens. This is not right, just stating a fact.

Later, it became the board's position that this was not our decision. If this was so important, they could change their bylaws. End of story.

Things seemed to be mellowing out. The ambience in the club felt good. The elections were over. Members were looking forward to the New Year and feeling that there was a balance in our future.

Well, the thirty-first of October arrived. I received a call at 5:30 p.m. from the agency stating that the temp had been dismissed. She had a few personal items in the office she needed to get. I said, "Get a list and we will have them for you. We would like to get our keys back as well." They said they would do that and be in contact the first of the week.

I had already spoken to our new accounting person about coming in on Monday, November 3, for an orientation of the job and to see our facility. She agreed to meet at the yacht club at 10:00 a.m.

I called the treasurer and audit person to be there as well. We met at 10:00 a.m. and started going over what the job entailed. The office was in major disarray. It appeared quite out of order. The temp was not exactly organized as one would expect of an accounting person.

Fortunately payroll had been done. Of course, we only had two employees, our bartenders. Checking the in basket, there were some invoices that needed paying. The new person seemed to have a handle on what was needed. It was obvious that there was a lot of work needed to get this place back in order. We gave her a tour of the facility and spent a little personal time getting a view of what she saw. At the end of a four-hour day, I sat down and had a one-on-one with her.

Everyone else had left. I explained a little more about our getting things in order. I said, "We are here to assist you in any way we can." She agreed to the challenge and to return on Wednesday at 10:00 a.m. to start her job. I told her time today would be included in her first paycheck. She said, "Thank you and see you Wednesday." I felt our first day had gone well.

On Wednesday, we all arrived at 10:00 a.m. except the new accounting person. At 10:15 a.m., I tried calling her cell phone. It went to voice mail. I left her a message. It was now 10:45 a.m. and there was no reply to my message. At 11:00 a.m., it did not appear as if this person was coming in. We tried doing a few things but made the decision to postpone any further efforts until later. I said I would follow up with this person and get back to them, meaning our people. I did try making contact with no response from this person. I even e-mailed her to respond even if she had decided not to take the job, no reply. Well, this was not what I was hoping for.

After returning home and the evening chores were done, I called a friend and asked for a meeting with her that evening. I shared the experience of that day with her. She asked if she might help. She was between things at the moment and had much experience in book-keeping in the restaurant trade. I said I would really appreciate a pair of fresh eyes looking at our situation. I knew this person as a friend as well as professionally.

I called the office team and said I would be returning on Thursday with a little help. They were on board with the idea. We were not going to be beaten by this challenge. It was apparent to me there was a mess in the office that needed major overhauling before seeking a person for the position.

CHAPTER 13

W E MET THE OTHERS AT the club only to find the computer down, the POS system not working properly, and various other barriers. There were many problems that needed to be attended to. After a frustrating day, it was time to head home and feed the horses. We headed out at about 2:30 p.m. and got about a mile from the club. My friend said she was not feeling well and needed to get some fresh air. I pulled over, and she got out and started walking. I thought to put the top down on my convertible. Maybe that would help. She got back in the car, and we drove a little further. She said, "Maybe I need something to drink. I still do not feel right." I stopped at a gas station with a store and fueled up while she got a drink. She was still feeling faint. She said this had happened once before and her husband had taken her to the emergency clinic. I called the office inquiring about the nearest one. After receiving that information, we headed there. I dropped her off and parked the car. I was in the waiting room for two hours before she returned. She had had an anxiety attack. Gee, I wonder what caused that. No wonder the other woman did not return.

It was now 5:00 p.m. Luckily, I was able to have a friend feed the horses. The traffic home was not too bad until we hit Santa Barbara. A few miles from our turnoff to Highway 154, traffic became stop and go. We were almost there when the car next to me apparently was not watching the car ahead of them. Instead of hitting the brakes, they hit the gas pedal and pushed the three cars ahead of them into each other. We looked at each other and said, "What the hell are we doing here?" By the time we turned on to Hwy 154, we had to laugh to keep from losing it. What a crazy day. I dropped my friend off at her truck and said, "See you in a few days." Enough was enough, and I felt lucky it was almost the weekend.

I received an e-mail from the commodore on Sunday, the ninth. It read,

> Last night the bar buzz was that our new book-keeper you hired showed up on Monday but has not been seen since. People have stopped by the office, but no one was there. So a simple question is, why have you not informed the Board of Directors? Twice I requested the board to approve hiring of the temp, but you and others said no.

I had no interest in responding to his e-mail. The treasurer did, and replying to his e-mail, said, "This is an inappropriate forum to discuss personnel issues. They are confidential and are Board Only issues."

His e-mail was cc'd to new board members for the next year as well as to others not involved. This was how he liked to stir the pot.

This same Sunday, on the ninth, I met my friend at our local watering hole and toasted with a margarita. We talked about the office and the financials. She still offered to help, so we made a plan, and I proposed it to the office team. We all agreed to what was needed to be done. We started fresh on Tuesday, and by Thursday, you could see light at the end of the tunnel. By Saturday evening, it seemed more like there was a skylight in the office, thanks to what I now referred to as the A-TEAM.

On Wednesday, the twelfth, I sent an e-mail to the treasurer. "Let's put something out to the board." After reading what I wrote, she asked if I minded she put in a few more comments. I said, "Please do." I usually had her check my releases before sending them. Always good to have a fresh pair of eyes to review what you are too close to. She crafted an e-mail that read,

> To all, due to the chaotic state of the office and after discussion with the vice commodore, the

audit person, and a few others, a decision was made to clean up the mess before trying to introduce a bookkeeper to the position. With the people's help who were on the process and procedures committee, we are now developing those polices as we move forward with our accounting and accountability in the office. The bills are being paid in a timely manner, and the bookkeeping is being corrected and cleaned up as well as being maintained. The bank provided our bar bags and did not charge for the accommodations.

Respectfully submitted,
The treasurer

We received thank-yous for the update from many directors.

The next week, I was told the person we had originally hired had contacted the office by e-mail requesting to be paid for the hours she worked. I approved and never was given any explanation of her not returning. Next, we did get our office keys back, and the temp's items were picked up in the exchange. Now I was receiving an e-mail from the temp agency that the commodore was inquiring about our inquiry on what happened. They wanted to know how to handle this. I said, "The next time he calls, you refer him to me. Let me know if this continues. He has already been informed that any further interference will not be tolerated."

Now that we were into the holidays, we would be working around each other's schedules and hoped to finish soon. In the meantime, everything was working like clockwork. We were hoping to have a permanent person by Monday, December 8. I would be keeping a tight rein on things from here on out. No rumors, just the facts.

I had put this information together for my monthly article to the membership. After the treasurer read it, it looked like this:

First off, I want to thank you for your vote of confidence in accepting me as your commodore for this next year. I feel with your support we're going to have a great year.

As your vice commodore, it is my responsibility to manage our office functions and financials. After returning from my leave of absence, I checked into exactly where we stood. I spoke to our audit person and she got me up to speed with the Audit Committee findings. We then developed a plan of attack so we could provide financials for the September Board of Directors Meeting, as well as the general meeting. This could not have never happened without the audit person's tenacity for perfection and her direction of our accounting person.

Other than that, I have been advised by our in-house lawyer that I cannot explain anything more than that—we are handling things. Trust me!

I would like to thank all our volunteers for their countless hours devoted to getting our club's business back on the straight and narrow. As the CFO and vice commodore and with the help of the board, we will make sure their efforts are not in vain.

Happy holidays!

I still had the resumes from my ad. We interviewed a woman who lived in an apartment complex close to our club. She had a lot of experience. I decided to hire her and see what happened. My friend would be able to get her started now that our office was up to snuff. On the third day, my friend stated that this person had a problem being directed by a younger person and was not listening to what she was being taught. She had her way of doing things. For me, this was not going to work. I met this person before she started the next day in the parking lot. She had a handful of papers and was telling me what she was going to do. We walked into the office, and I said, "This is not working for me. You are not going to come in here and take over. You need to listen and adapt to what it is you're doing. I do not think that is possible. This is a member's club and you need to understand that." She said she would try changing. I said, "I have your check for the hours you have worked, and I appreciate your time. I think it best we part company now." She looked a little perplexed by what I said. It was nothing personal, just for the better.

She thought for a minute and said, "I do have another job, and he wants me to work more hours. It is coming time for the tax season." I gave her the check and offered her a hug. We hugged, and I walked her out of the building.

A moment later, she was knocking at the door. She said, "You forgot to sign my paycheck." I signed it, and she was off.

The next person was younger and interested, but something did not seem right. There was another young woman who had shown interest much earlier in the beginning. She had some accounting experience. She was a food and beverage server that knew what a POS (point of sale) system was and how it worked. All the accounting people knew QuickBooks but not about a POS system. I connected her to my friend, and they worked together for a week. My friend said, "This is the one—she is sharp and learns fast." This job was only part-time so she could easily work both if she wanted to. This person worked under my friend as a temp until we knew she would be the one for the position. She was hired as our employee after the first of the year. She is now employed with the club as our bookkeeper.

After that, my friend was available by phone when questions needed answers and would come down once a month until it was no longer necessary. We had also retained a nonprofit CPA to guide us in the proper direction. With the issues from the previous year and continuing into the next year, I felt it was important to have sound advice and that they be familiar with our process for tax time.

As the vice commodore, I was responsible for making sure all people in charge and those events went well, also making sure the cleaning company was in tune with our calendar to keep the club clean for any and all events. November was a busy month. Our annual award banquet was on the second Saturday of November. This was a dinner and awards ceremony for the commodore to thank all of those who deserved recognition for their service. There were trophies and awards of all kinds. This dinner would be prepped by our men's cooking group. I was lead chef, and it all went well. The next Saturday was a chili cook-off and social, meaning entertainment. The following Saturday was the annual angler's awards and scampi dinner also being cooked by the men's cooking group. There were the awards for the angler's big fish, men's tournament, women's tournament, etc. The raffles supported our White Sea Bass Grow Out program. It would be quite the night.

On Tuesday, the eighteenth, before the angler's dinner, there was our last board of directors meeting for business until next year. The last meeting in December, it was customary for the commodore to take the board out for dinner for their service for that year. This November meeting was an important one because we were trying to tie up business until the Change of Watch, which was the second Saturday of January.

The meeting was called to order, and we got down to the business at hand. The new board was again invited to listen but did not participate. Their turn would be next year. I did give a thorough report on the office progress. I shared all the trials and tribulations and stated we were on course. The commodore was particularly pleased since this happened in his year. After thanking me for our efforts, I reminded him that his actions almost collapsed our accounting system and he was not the one involved in its resurrection.

One item on the agenda was from a past commodore who wanted to know the status of our lease extension. Our lease was to come to an end in June of next year. With no knowledge of where we stood, it prevented the club making further plans for the future. A letter was to be sent to our main lease holder requesting our interest in the extension. The commodore had proposed a letter, but it was never approved by the board. We understood a letter had been sent and were interested in seeing a copy. The commodore refused to provide a copy. After citing the bylaws, the commodore was told to produce a copy for the office by the next day before 6:00 p.m. He agreed.

After finishing up with board business, it was time once again to call for a closed session, once again calling for a short recess and excusing the new members and anyone else not on the immediate board. The closed session was now in session. There were three items on the agenda. The first was about a complaint filed by a director's wife complaining about a member badgering her about her husband. This complaint was filed and read in a closed session in April. The commodore said he would handle it. He did not follow up and resolve this complaint. Instead, it blew up in our October general meeting when the director made allegations to this person, when she had no knowledge of what he was referring to. The commodore brought a complaint against the director for his outburst. It was then brought before the board to be sustained or not. It was voted "not sustained" since the commodore failed to handle the original complaint in a timely matter. The vote was seven nays and one abstained.

The commodore made a formal complaint against me for signing and handing a final payroll check to the accounting person for her dismissal. She was fired on June 30 with no warning. After a lengthy discussion, I explained that I was given full authority to handle this whole accounting mess by the board at our meeting in July. I felt she should be granted one final monthly check for her services following the employee code. This action was voted on. The judge advocate agreed that my actions were appropriate. Was there enough evidence to sustain this complaint? The vote was four nays, three abstained, and one director walked out of the room and left the building.

The next complaint made was against the commodore for allowing the temp to continue working during the period of September 1 to September 16 after quitting the agency and not notifying the board of his action. It was found sustained. The vote was five yays, two nays, and I abstained. In an effort to resolve this matter without any more negativity and keep the club running as smoothly as possible, an agreement was reached. The commodore promised to be more transparent and not take any action without approval from the board, and this included communication with our landlord, lease letter, etc. The commodore again promised to get the letter back to the office for safekeeping. The commodore and the vice commodore shook hands as confirmation of the agreement. Before the meeting was adjourned, it was stated that a copy of a W-9 form with the temp's signature dated 9/1 had been found in the office during its overhaul. No further action was necessary. The meeting was adjourned.

I called the treasurer the next morning to see what was going on. I asked if all was well. She replied it was OK. It sounded there was something up. "Is everything good?"

She said, "I am talking to a person who works for the land management company that we lease from. He told her that the main office in Dana Point asked them not to engage in any further conversation about our pending lease option. They will contact us when the time comes." Again this went back to the commodore for his involvement.

I said, "I have no problem with that. This will keep the commodore from eroding this relationship any further. I will handle things when contacted next year."

The next day, the commodore sent an e-mail out, refusing to comply with last night's agreement to bring the letter to the office. Several directors replied stating, "Just do as you were asked and agreed to."

I found this hard to believe he had sent this e-mail to the new board as well. This was outright embarrassing. Even after the outcome of the closed session last night. I responded to his e-mail:

> And my dog has Fleas. So why are you taking a stand you cannot and will not win? This is about the club. You are not the Grand Dragon. You work for the Board, so give this up like normal thinking person would or face the consequences. It is as simple as that. As I stated last night, put your hands under your legs and be a figurehead. Meaning you make no decision without board approval. This is not your decision to make, or there will be action taken. Do you really think

going before the general membership will give
you credence? I guess you forgot who was in the
audience at the September and October meetings.

I was far from the only person that thought the commodore
was not fit for the job. I said, "I told the rear commodore, when he
pushed me for an apology to the membership for my presentation at
the September meeting because he got one or two e-mails in regards
to this. I will leave it up to the membership before I apologize. After
being voted the commodore, I did apologize to anyone offended. I
also explained what I said was to be directed to the board, not the
membership. To be honest, it was directed at you. If you do not follow the rules of engagement, you will cause chaos. So what you are
doing for the benefit of the Yacht Club as an individual, thinking
you're doing us a favor, when it is only you being a micromanager
and not a team player? Stand down like you said you would last night
or face the music. It saddens me for the new members of the board to
be exposed to such ridiculousness. I feel they felt their involvement
would be of a more professional manner, not such a petty state of
affairs. I hope they will be able to overlook this and join me and the
board to move our yacht club forward and have a rewarding and
productive year."

He did finally surrender the letter.

Now it was Saturday, the twenty-second. It was the angler's
scampi dinner to be cooked by our group. I did not attend the dinner. I believed it was sold out.

I was spending as much time with Sally as she would allow. She
was in a lot of pain. We would share a meal and watch old movies on
TV until she would fall asleep on my lap. One of the few chores she
asked me to do was light up her medical marijuana and smoke it for
her so she would get a little relief from her pain. She liked the fumes
but did not like to smoke it herself. I felt it was the least I could do.
She had a doctor's appointment soon to find out what was going to
be the next step. It is hard to watch someone you love slip away. You
just do what you can during the time you have.

The next morning, I was checking my e-mail. I noticed I had one from my friend who was in charge of the men's cooking group. I figured it was an update on the event. Well, it was, but it was not what I expected.

It read,

> As of tonight, I'm no longer a member of this cooking group. I went to El Hefe no.1 tonight and I asked if he received my e-mail about updating our trophy in the downstairs trophy case, also choosing an outstanding member of the year from our group. This person never says no and has helped on most dinners this year. I thought the people on that trophy were members who have stepped up and gave 100 percent. Then I mentioned the name of the person who has agreed to step into my shoes for next year, and then El Hefe started going ballistic on me. He was telling me that I couldn't pick anyone. I had no say in anything and he was head of this group. He will choose who will be the USC and he will do what he wants with the trophy and I'm basically nothing, he is in charge. After being yelled at and he was so furious, I asked him, "Why are you so mad at me?" His reply was, "You do what I want. I'm in charge, not you." I handed him my apron and said, "You fucking cook, I'm done." An hour later, he asked me for my resignation by tomorrow. I sent it to him by my phone as soon as he left. I also told him he could do the upcoming dinners. I'm not. Anyway, I'm done! He gave me the navy guy's name and his phone number.

I was not expecting this. This man had been the USC for our group since January and got treated like this in November at our last meal excluding the holiday dinners for the navy and coast guard.

Well, being the former USC from last year and now the incoming commodore, this was on my shoulders. A point that must be understood is the cooking group was started in 2003 by El Hefe no.1, as he referred to himself. Some others in this group you would refer to as the old guard. Our present commodore was a member of this group, along with a few other characters. What I am getting at was the gentleman El Hefe asked to resign was also a director on the board, and four days prior to this evening, he had voted to sustain the complaint against the commodore in a closed-session meeting. Closed-session meetings were not to be discussed beyond that room. Well, it looked to me this was a little payback.

It was time to take this matter to hand. Obviously El Hefe did not come to or was not listening when I gave my presentation to become commodore and did not see the emasculator I held up to show how we removed things that get in the way.

I decided to send an e-mail over his bow first.

Dear El Hefe,

I receive the following e-mail (in which I attached a copy) from our USC (Ultimate Supreme Commander), which you dubbed him at our Change of Watch the beginning of this year. It does not settle well with me to hear he was asked to resign from his post for recommending a future USC and his recommendation for the person most deserving for their participation cooking this year. The USC has done more than his share upholding the standards of this group. I am saddened that he has surrender his resignation.

I believe you owe him an apology! You told me as the USC for my year that whatever I said was to be interpreted as the word for that year. I conveyed those words to him believing they were true. You may be the creator of this group; however, you cannot control it, you must nurture it. Seeing yourself, as your picture reflects, the Buddha of this group. This group cannot continue without supporters that believe in the cause or it will die, becoming a fond memory.

The scheduled events for end of the year are December 12 for the UWDT, who have requested an Italian Buffet. And December 20 for the Coast Guard, which is already headed up by a member. They are buying the food, and we are responsible for cooking, serving, and cleanup.

Since the USC has resigned, and you have taken back the reins by your actions, let the incoming vice commodore know how you are handling these events.

Awaiting a response, choose it wisely. The future of your group is at "Steak."

To refer back to El Hefe, to him being the Buddha, I received an award, which was a medal with his picture on one side, and the back side said "Lifetime Achievement Award for BBQ Technology. You have raised the bar." I had built a wood-burning metal barbecue for our group. His picture was him sitting in the Buddha position. I hope he was wearing white skivvies along with his glasses and nothing else. You cannot really tell if he was wearing anything with his legs crossed and stomach hanging over.

There was no immediate response to my e-mail, so I decided to give my resignation to this group.

Moving on. After reading the USC's e-mail, I was shocked and unaware of any politics within the order of this group. I was under the impression the order as deemed was for fun!

I would be stepping down from any post I may presumably hold and be joining my friend in the audience. I did not need validation in order to cook. The reward was in a clean plate and making hungry, appreciative people happy.

We would continue to cook quality meals at affordable prices and make the club some income. I appreciated their support.

I became responsible for the UWDT dinner and prepared all the menu requested in house for sixty-eight people. They said sixty people until the morning of the event, and then it grew to seventy. It all went well, and they were very happy.

I finally received a reply on December 7, Pearl Harbor Day, at 3:46 p.m. from El Hefe. The USC was sent the same e-mail. The USC replied at 4:50 p.m. that same day. We would not go into it. I believed his reply would be considered self-explanatory and hot to the touch. After reading both, I decided to reply to El Hefe and cc the USC.

El Hefe's reply read,

> I am sorry for the belated reply to your e-mail on 24 November. I have made several attempts to reach you and the USC, but my calls have been unanswered. My wife and I have had numerous medical, financial, and social issues to deal with over the past days, and I am just getting around to answering my mail.
>
> First and foremost, I too am surprised and deeply saddened regarding your and the USC's e-mail and apologize for any perceived misunderstandings.
>
> Second, I also am truly sorry that he has chosen to resign as USC. He chose to resign. I did not ask him to resign. What I did do if he, indeed, chose to resign, was I asked him to put his resignation in writing so that the group could arrange for his successor.
>
> Third, I did tell both you and him that each was responsible for the management and leadership of the group under the Prolog lemma for each of your years respectively. I have never challenged or criticized your leadership during your terms.

Fourth, yes, I am the creator of this group, the founder, the FUSC. I wrote the Prololglemma—the rules by which all members swear to and abide by. And yes, since 2003, I have had no control over this group. I have no wish or authority to control the group. They will survive and thrive as a function of the quality and wisdom of their leadership.

Fifth, I have not and will not take over the reins of the group. As you know, by Faire no. 7, the replacement of the current USC is the responsibility of the previous year's membership committee and its foreman. In this case, it is your membership committee that is responsible for his replacement.

Sixth, the real disagreement between him and me was that he did not appoint a membership committee in early October to find new apprentices and nominate the USC for the next year as Faire no.7 prescribes.

Peace in our time.
El Hefe

CHAPTER 14

M Y RESPONSE WAS SHORT AND to the point. Answering each of his numbered explanation:

First, your reply to this event is late in response. Sorry, you are having issues. My girlfriend is dying, and I still find time to deal with real issues at her request. Sorry, so no excuses.

Second, you asked him to resign.

Third, you made a verbal statement about us being in charge. You said he was not up to it, and I stated the he was and would make sure he was successful.

Fourth, stating you started this group but do not control or run the organization. Why would you demand a resignation without the authority of those you say do.

Fifth, if you are not running this group and it is by whom ever you gave the authority to what you did?

Sixth, I was not appointed before a board as the new USC. I selected the USC and introduced my candidate to you, and I stated after your comments about him that I would make sure it would be a smooth transition.

And on that note, he did announce at our meeting in August a new USC who later decided to decline. So we decided on a new nominee whom we felt was qualified and would back up his performance whenever necessary. That is what people do. You were not present at either meeting in April or August for the bonding meetings.

Well, El Hefe made one more reply saying, "I am deeply saddened and perplexed regarding the current circumstances within our group. I am tom between pursuing what I believe to be a just cause and acting in a manner that is not in the best interest of the group.

"As the founder of this organization, I am proud of the one hundred men who have served diligently, dutifully, and merrily in support of our Yacht Club during the past fourteen years, but it is now evident that my consul and assistance is neither needed nor desired. Therefore, I hereby stand down and instruct the organizations scribe to immediately remove my name from the role of active in this group.

"Best wishes to all, El Hefe number 1."

I had one last statement: "Gee, El Hefe number 1, that is your baby, not mine. I have already given you my answer on the twenty-fourth of November with your failing to reach out and undo the wrong you did. This is not my torch to carry.

"They did the Coast Guard dinner and called me three days before the UWDT dinner and stated they would cook that dinner. I said thanks, but I have already bought the ingredients. This meal is being cooked from scratch. What these people do for our country, deserve whatever meal they have asked for. It is my duty to honor their request. Thanks anyway."

Well, if this seems shocking to anyone reading this, I was not surprised at all. I had been watching people for quite some time. All I can say to this is I was happy to be at the helm when the storm started brewing and able to contend with it as it happened and was there to serve what was necessary to say at that time. The organization more or less collapsed. The old guard held to their declaration. Their membership mostly dissolved. No more dinners prepared by this group were on the calendar for the next year. This was to be my year as the commodore, and some questions needed to be answered before I would allow them to rally again.

HEY! .... HEY! .... HEY!

THE
BEEFEATERS

A Collegial Men's Cooking Group

PROFORMA:

1. Prepare & Serve Dinners Monthly
2. Focus on Ambiance, Presentation and Quality
3. Promote: Cooking Science & Kitchen Skills
4. Develop: Menus, Budgets, Shopping and Promotion
5. Develop: Food Health & Safety Protocols

FINANCIAL: $766.00 – Bank Balance 6/2015

MEMBERSHIP FEE: $50.00 / year

SUBSCRIPTION: COOK's Illustrated Magazine

BONDING MEETINGS: Quarterly

It was now December. The club was being decorated for the upcoming holiday events. It was now time for the tree-lighting ceremony, parade of lights, and special holiday dinners.

Well, Sally had her doctor's appointment, and it was said the clock was ticking, and we needed to admit her and prepare her for hospice. The short story, preparing her so she can be managed to be taken care of easily. She would soon have no control of what her body was doing. That was a hard thing to swallow. Now just the facts—Sally was in a great deal of pain when she was admitted. Her doctor was unavailable to prescribe anything, so it just continued. There was no way to sleep when nurses were constantly coming and going and changing shifts. It was exhausting, to say the least.

After the colostomy operation, they now had to start her drip to control the pain. She was one strong woman. The only company she wanted was my presence. She would be furious with those that invaded her space thinking they could cheer her up. Once on the drip, she would fade in and out. I would just sit to be there. It was coming time for her to be released to hospice. I was not being given any information. I assumed she was coming back to the valley to her place.

She just disappeared without me having any knowledge of where she was going. I finally got her twin brother's e-mail address. A client of mine worked with him. He was in his office saying he went to visit his sister in Santa Ynez. My client was listening to his story. He said his sister introduced this guy she had been dating, who lived across the street from her place on a horse ranch. Nice guy, he made a special meatloaf that day and sent it home with us. He shared a few more details with my client, and she asked, "Where is this ranch?" He told her my name and the name of the ranch.

She said, "That is the ranch my horse is retired on." She later shared that story with me. Months later led me to asking her for his information to see what he knew about his sister.

It turned out Sally was moved to a friend's home on the beach in a gated community above Ventura. At that point, I would text her messages to see if she would respond. Days later, I finally received a text message from her. She was OK but was not interested in visitors, not even me. Well, all you can do is what has been asked of you. I texted her, and she would reply when she was up to it. We finally spoke on the phone, and it was great to hear her voice. After several attempts, I was finally able to make a date to stop by. I was only to stop when I was to be at the yacht club. Of course, I lied and said I was coming through the next day. It was whatever it took to get to see her again. It was a beautiful home and location. They set up a bed in the living room. You could see the ocean and hear the surf. She was very thin but looked good. She was walking around and even taking short walks on the beach. She had been taken there by ambulance. No sirens, just a precaution. It was felt that she would not live much longer. The priest was brought in twice and both times, and she said, "I am not ready to go." Once out of the hospital, she was finally able to sleep without being disturbed. She began feeling stronger and was more determined to stick around. I was allowed to visit when she asked me. What ended up happening was she got a little better and outlasted her time frame there. The remodeling of this home was put on hold, so Sally would have a pleasant place to stay before passing away. It was now determined that she was going to have to move out and return to her place in Santa Ynez. Her cancer was far from remission, but her mind was driving her forward. She moved back to the valley and continued her fight to live another day.

My last event I was to be responsible for was the New Year's Eve dinner. The music had already been booked. I had hired a caterer who also had a restaurant in the harbor. We were friends, and I was going to help making sure the prime rib was perfect. This crowd was a picky one even if everything was right. That way they could blame me, not them. I made sure that the seating went well. There were a few hiccups, but that was why I was overseeing everything. This was my final task and was not going to let anything dealing with my part fail. When the food started getting served, I left the building. Sally was not up for company, so I just headed home and called it a night.

CHAPTER 15

NOW I WAS THE COMMODORE. The first thing the commodore does is bless the fleet. This event is called the commodore's cruise, which is the first Saturday of January. Our fleet from the membership gathered on the inside of the break water at the entrance of the harbor. A theme is chosen by the commodore. Mine was Buckaroo Buccaneer. The commodore, vice commodore, and rear commodore dressed appropriately. We were taken out in an electric boat, and I blessed each boat with a prayer and gave the captain a bottle of champagne. Well, my outfit was a black leather duster, black motorcycle boots, white pirate shirt, and a black cowboy hat with three sides folded up to be a pirate's hat sporting a embroidered star from one of my favorite wineries in Paso Robles.

It was a fun traditional event. Afterward, we returned to the club for libation and a light lunch. It was a great way to start the year and celebrate a new beginning. The outgoing commodore came into the bar. I thought it was appropriate that I say hi and shake his hand. He shook my hand and said, "It is all yours now. Don't F it up." I thought to myself as I was walking away, *Well, that bar has been raised too high for that to happen.* I would not have expected anything more from him.

The next event was the second Saturday of the month, which was the Change of Watch dinner, ceremony, and dance. Usually this event was put together by the outgoing commodore. But since I asked him to put his hands underneath his legs, I would become the one in charge. Normally the men's cooking group would do this dinner, but they were disbanded by their own doing. My friend who was the ousted USC offered to do the menu and cooked the dinner. I hired a member's band to play dance music. I had one request, and that was they had to play "Happy Days Are Here Again." It was a great dinner, a short ceremony, and good music. It was a great evening for all of those who attended.

As the outgoing commodore, it was customary to be asked if they would like to be inducted into an organization for past commodores. I had seen an e-mail that was sent about this commodore being inducted into that organization. I believed you needed to be of good character in order to become a member. The founder was Ev. G. Henry, commodore of the Rainer Yacht Club in Seattle, Washington, in 1953. It has grown from a humble beginning to a worldwide organization. It is called the International Order of the Blue Gavel with a membership of over four thousand past commodores worldwide. It is amazing that the idea of one outgoing commodore resulted in an organization of outstanding individuals of distinction and latitude and, by their actions, receive the respect of the yachting society throughout the world.

Am I missing something here? I thought character meant something good about someone. Why would you pollute this organization with bad character? I guess I did miss something.

I did speak to our parliamentarian about this, concerning our past commodore. Even though he knew about most of what this commodore did during his term, they still decided to induct this individual into this organization. How could that be? It turned out the parliamentarian was our IOBG district director, and another member of our club who is now serving as our commodore was president of our district. Maybe that is how it works.

The IOBG bylaws state in Article II Section 1. "(A) To selectively associate ladies and gentlemen of good character, having a common love and appreciation of yachting, social and outdoor activities of every kind, on the basis of background, character, personality and social acceptability."

I think I have made my point.

The day after the Change of Watch the gentleman who became vice commodore left for over two weeks for Norway. He would not be present for the first board meeting, I had my bases already covered since the accounting problems had been handled, and we had hired and trained a solid person for that position. My friend was still available and helping fine-tune for this year and getting the tax information to the CPA for the previous year. I had my treasurer and secretary from the year before who had been involved with everything we did, so we were a good working team. This made for a foundation for a smooth transition into a new year.

Chapter 16

I T WAS TIME FOR MY first board meeting as the commodore and the presiding officer of the meetings. One of our members asked to be on the agenda. He addressed his thoughts that our in-house publication be mailed to each member. This item seemed to be discussed every few years. Depending on the audience, it went one way or the other. This gentleman was of the old school of thought and wanted a paper copy to be sent out. Last time this was approached, those that wanted it paid for its mailing, and the rest liked it electronically sent and read it online. We entertained the idea, but this had to be approved by the membership. It was moved to the agenda for the general meeting at the end of the week. Everything else on the agenda was a little simpler. I did have to call for a closed session to discuss a problem that had been disclosed to me. I called for a closed session to discuss a phone message the office had received pertaining to an invoice that had been personally delivered to the coast guard office. The commanding officer had left a message that someone from our yacht club had delivered a handwritten invoice for $750 from our yacht club for services rendered by our club for doing their annual holiday dinner. I wanted to inform the board that this was not from our office but delivered by one of the members of the men's cooking group. The coast guard had purchased the food, and this group was to cook and serve it. In the past, the yacht club has always waived the rental fee and donated the linen as part of our being a nonprofit, especially for these people. I was furious about this—just another reason this group self-imploded living up to the standards they created. I asked the treasurer to please contact the coast guard and apologize. This was a terrible mistake and would not happen again and to go over and get a copy of this invoice for our records. I asked the board for permission to send the coast guard an official apology letter to be signed by me. It was agreed upon. I also stated to the board, board business is board business. I did not want it discussed in the bar. The closed session was adjourned, but our regular meeting was not adjourned. It was extended due to the annual budget for the year was incomplete. I was awaiting data that had not been available, so I asked that our meeting resume at 6:30 p.m. before the general meeting. I needed to present my budget to the board for approval before the general meeting. The meeting was accepted to be extended until that time. The letter was written to the coast guard by the secretary, I signed it, and it was mailed to the commanding officer with my apology. I had hoped they would be returning for their event during my year as commodore and gave my personal guarantee that there would be no further incidents on my watch.

It was now the time for general meeting. Our extended session was called, and I presented my budget for the year and it was approved the meeting was adjourned. It was now time for the general meeting. It went well. The gentlemen who wanted our publication delivered to all members addressed the membership. There was much discussion, and the subject seemed to trade positions from no to yes, depending on the audience. This time it was to be in favor of everyone receiving a copy and approved by the membership who was present. This item expense was not calculated in my budget. The cost was $220 per mailing per month, and a $220 annual fee for bulk mailing. That was $2,860 that affected the budget I just proposed to the membership that was approved twenty minutes earlier before this conversation. That was the highlight of the evening. That debate was a little contested, but they won this time. The meeting was adjourned. Retiring to the bar, I was asked by members who did not attend the meeting how it went. I gave a short version of the meeting. When I said they would be getting a copy of our publication in the mail, it was stated that they thought that had been resolved two years ago. I stated that is why it was important to attend our meetings. Things change, and it depends on those attending how the outcome will be.

CHAPTER 17

THERE WERE MEALS PREPARED TO finish out our monthly dinners. The next big deal was our Super Bowl tailgate party.

It was now February, and the first fell on a Sunday, which was Super Bowl. It was a big event with great food and camaraderie. It was always a full house.

I was expecting to hear from our landlord about our lease extension. It was usually considered automatic, but there were some issues that have occurred over the past ten years that needed resolution. As a director in 2013 then becoming vice commodore in 2014, it appeared if I were to continue on as commodore this would be a situation I and my board would have to contend with. I never thought I would be putting myself in this negotiation process. When I started as a director, my term would be up, and I would not be dealing with this. I was not sure of what this all meant. This was never disclosed by our audit committee because they never looked that deep.

The past commodore had inflamed our relationship with this item when he was pursuing it without the board's knowledge. This was a waiting game. I was contacted by the now past commodore that their agent wanted my phone number. They were ready to talk about our catch-up fees. I received a call from their local office in our harbor that their representative was trying to contact me. I was then told to call him on the next day, February 9, at 10:00 a.m. to discuss the matter. I did call, making contact. He said I would be receiving by mail their findings on the catch-up fees, as they were referred to. These were fees that had not been paid in the past ten-year lease. These would have to be resolved before a lease extension would be considered. I thought to myself, *What a lucky guy I am. What have I inherited?*

I did receive the document disclosing the catch-up fees, which had been calculated by a reputable firm in the Los Angeles area. The catch-up charges included the CPI increases on the security deposit, the monthly rent, and the common area charges that had not been applied to our rent for the past ten years. In 2012, it was disclosed by the commodore that we had not been paying the common area cost, so that started being paid in July of 2012 at $200 per month. Those monies had already been deducted from the total we now owed. We had overpaid the electric payments by $4,961 over the past ten years, leaving our total of catch-up fees at $41,200. This is the total we owed and needed to resolve before a lease extension would be agreed to.

I was a little shocked at the total, but it was what it was. There had been some discussion in the past about how we might deal with this, but this was a sizeable amount of money. We had money in a savings account but not that much. It was once stated that they could only go back four years due to the statute of limitation. Maybe or maybe not. This was our landlord, and if not handled correctly, we could lose our lease. I was not willing to give this information out. Only a few were privy, and only those who would not leak this out until our board meeting. This was to be discussed in a closed session. When the gentlemen called the past commodore for my phone number, the past commodore requested a copy. When I spoke to the representative, he mentioned the past commodore's request for a copy. I said, "Absolutely not." I was the commodore, and I would release this information in a closed session at the board meeting. He was a director now and had no authority to request anything without my approval. Two days after receiving my copy of the catch-up fees the past commodore called the representative wanting to know where his copy was. The representative sent an e-mail to me about that request. I replied if he asked again to refer him to me. He was not to receive a copy. That was the end of that.

It was now time for our February board meeting. All were present, but the past commodore who was now a director. He was serving his second year of his two-year obligation on the board and now as a director with a vote. Our meeting went well, not too much on the agenda. I had put a closed session on my agenda to discuss the catch-up fees. It was now time for that closed session to be called. It was announced that only board members would stay and anyone else would now need to leave the room. Once secured, the door was locked and this session was called to order. I said I have been contacted by our landlord's people and I needed to disclose what our catch-up fees are. There were three new directors who really did not know anything about this issue. The others had knowledge but nothing more than that. I explained that over the past ten years, there was a cost of living percentage that had not been applied to our annual security deposit. That amount is $1,663. The cost of living increase was $27,740 on the rent. At that point, I was getting some reaction out of the board. I said I was not done yet. There was also $16,600 owed for the common area maintenance, which was $200 a month. The complete total of catch-up fees was $46,003. You can imagine what the new board members were thinking: *How did this happen? I did not sign up for this. I have only been a member for two years.* I said, "Wait a minute, I am not done yet. The good news is we overpaid our electric bill, so we can deduct $4,961 from those fees. Also we have been paying the common area fees of $200 since July of 2012. We have been credited that money. The amount we owe now is $41,200. With that being said, we will not be discussing this tonight. This needs to be thought about because the outcome of this solution affects our lease extension for the next ten years. This needs to be negotiated properly and with some thought before we put our cards on the table." The conversation stated was, "I said there will be no comment tonight. We will talk about this at the next board meeting in closed session. I have only had this information for a few days. I am still thinking on how might be best way to go forward. Please turn in the information I have provided to you. I believe you have enough in your head to think about. This information is not to be discussed with anyone except another board member. Do you understand?" I received their confirmation on my request. I asked if someone would please make a motion to adjourn for I had nothing further to discuss. A motion was made to adjourn the meeting and it received a second. I said, "This meeting is adjourned and thank you." I got that done in fifteen minutes, which I thought was great. If this had happened last year, we would still be in the room. After last year's meetings, I made a decision to limit time speaking by each person. There would be one person talking at one time. I purchased a one-minute and a three-minute hourglasses. If you cannot make your point in that time frame, then say what you mean and mean what you say. I hate wasting my time. These meetings should not be more than an hour.

I was not getting much feedback from those I trusted with this information. Five days later, I was receiving calls and e-mail from the representative about what I thought and he wanted to schedule a meeting. I spoke to the treasurer and the judge advocate about his request. They both agreed this had to go before the board first. The representative persisted on having a meeting. I contacted the treasurer and judge advocate again and said maybe we should have a meeting to discuss matters before our board meeting so we would have more insight to what they're thinking. It was not like we refused to pay the increases, they were never applied over the past ten years. We paid what our monthly invoice statement stated. When it was realized we in default in 2012 the now treasurer was a director then. She was asked by the commodore at that time to contact their general manager about the common area charges of $200 per month. He never replied to her calls. The $200 was then paid each month from that time on. After my conversation, the treasurer and judge advocate agreed on having a meeting with this gentleman. I called the representative and agreed to meet. I suggested a neutral place. He chose a restaurant in Fillmore halfway between locations. I accepted his offer. The judge advocate was unavailable, so I asked the treasurer if she would accompany me to this meeting. She agreed, so I confirmed the meeting.

We were early and ordered iced tea. A margarita sounded better because we were in a Mexican restaurant. Our meeting was scheduled for three o'clock. A few minutes later, an older gentlemen in a light-colored suit came in. I figured it was him. We introduced ourselves and sat down. First it was light conversation, and he told us who he was and what he had done in his career in real estate development. He was a father in-law to the owner of our marina, and they held the master lease.

He was brokering this resolution for them. We did not give much personal information. After talking about our yacht club and the facility, it was obvious he had not seen our club and was unfamiliar with yacht clubs. No matter we were here to discuss our situation.

He had a yellow pad and pen. He said, "We are willing to drop the CPI on the security deposit." It was $1,663. He asked, "What about the common area fees? I don't have those figures, but—"

I interrupted and said, "I do, they're $16,600. I think we should pay the complete amount. Those fees are out of your pocket. They were paid inclusively in your monthly fees in your master lease."

He then stated, "What about the rent increase, the cost of living over the past ten years?"

I said, "That is $27,740, I would suggest that we split that. That would be $13,870 each. The CPI was never applied to our rent over the past ten years. Had that happened, we would not be in this situation. I cannot say yes or no to what we have discussed, but at least we have had a conversation." He agreed, and we adjourned our meeting. He left and paid for our dinners we had ordered after he arrived. He chose not to eat, just a glass of tea.

I thought the discussion went well. I was just a little surprised he had not brought anything but the pen and pad to the meeting. On the way back to the club, I was discussing the meeting with the treasurer. I asked what she thought. She was not sure, but we had at least made an effort. I said if what we discussed could be agreed upon I felt that proposed deal should be good for our relationship with the marina and secure our lease extension for the next ten years. She was not as optimistic. I said, "I do not want to start playing hard ball. What we had offered reduced our catch-up fees by $15,533. We would then owe $25,509 instead of the $41,200. I thought I could sell that to the board. We had a little over $30,000 in a savings account. I guess we will have to see what the board has to say." I was not interested in having a special meeting.

A few days later, the gentleman from the meeting called and requested that I submit in writing what we had discussed. I said I could not, that this needed to go before the board. He then contacted the office and asked the treasurer to put this in writing and send it to him. She contacted me. I said I would handle it. I again reminded him our meeting was not until March 17 and he would have to wait until then. He stopped calling us.

CHAPTER 18

OR THE MONTH OF FEBRUARY, our activities were our usual Wednesday night dinners, which included bingo if there were enough members interested. Thursdays, the bar was open and it was movie night. Friday was happy hour. One Friday a month would be a birthday bash celebrating those with birthdays and anniversaries. We had a fish fry every few months on a Friday. Then there were our Saturday night dinners and sometimes socials, meaning entertainment or dancing. This month we would be celebrating Valentine's Day. It was always well attended.

Sally and I would be celebrating at her place. This was the anniversary of her operation, so we were lying low for the evening sharing a meal, a movie, and a kiss for dessert. She now needed assistance at this time. A nurse would come by and check on her and make sure she was taking her medication. She was doing well, but this was for precautionary purposes. She did not like the fact that her space was being invaded.

The Midwinter's Race event remained at our club. All went well, and the ceremonies went off without any problems. I made sure I was present to visit with the past commodore who attended and presented the awards last year. She was also the presenter this year. We had a guest who was also a presenter who arrived in a wheelchair. The access to our upstairs dining and bar area was not accessible. We had a chairlift on our outside stairway that had to be removed because it fell out of compliance with state requirements. It had been removed. We were waiting for our lease to get settled before we could address that problem. I and another member offered to cross our arm and lock hands together providing fireman's chair to assist her up the stairway. She accepted our offer sitting in between our arms and lifted her up the stairs, while her husband carried her chair upstairs. We aimed to please. The lift would be the next thing to deal with once our lease was secured.

I had been deliberating the best way to go about negotiating the catch-up fees and get this directed with the board. As a rancher and one dealing with horses, you become a high-fiber management engineer. In layman's terms, horse manure. Picking pens would seem tedious and a waste of one's valuable time. But when you are struggling with an issue of a mind-provoking magnitude, it is a great thing to be doing. You are going through the motions, but your mind is relaxed so you can focus on an issue while not being bothered by anyone. So I found the time I was looking for to work out how I would move forward with this dilemma of the catch-up fees to resolve this, and the lease would be in hand. So our hands would no longer be tied, preventing us from doing what we need to do as a club moving forward.

It was now March, which was a very busy month anyway. Our opening days were usually the first Sunday of April, but this year it was Easter Sunday. So it would be the following Sunday. It was our turn to get all the invitations out for all the yacht clubs in the Association of Santa Barbara Channel Yacht Clubs. This happened every seven years. Fortunately, our secretary and treasurer were up for this task. Our yacht club was to be cleaned and shined for the opening day ceremonies. We had shipshape cleaning every Saturday until then. Everything needed to be done was done by our members. These tasks were delegated and completed. In-house work was overseen by the vice commodore. He lucked out this year because our landlord's maintenance crew was doing all the exterior work like painting and repairs. These were things previously done by us for our opening day. Since we were working diligently on solving our catch-up fees, they were supporting our cause.

The first Saturday dinner was one of our favorites. It was the annual angler's lobster dinner. This was normally done by the men's cooking group, but they had disbanded. It was handled by the people who supported the White Sea Bass Grow Out program, and all proceeds went to this program.

The next was the Saint Patrick's Day celebration with corned beef and cabbage with Irish dancers as the entertainment. A fun time for all!

I was starting to get phone calls and e-mail from the representative again. He was saying I needed to get something to him. The owner was going to South America, where he had other business for two weeks. He said this person wanted to get this done before leaving, so I needed to submit something now, before the weekend. He had a meeting with him on Saturday. Our board meeting was a week away. I said again I would have to review this with the board. I did not want to call for a special meeting. He again stated his facts. So I said, "Let me put something together and I will let you know." With the next morning being Wednesday, I put on my high-fiber engineer's hat or cowboy hat and proceeded cleaning pens. I was reviewing in my mind all I knew and had heard over the past two and a half years on this subject of being in default due to these fees. I kept thinking, *How did this happen? We were $41,200 in the rears*. I remember the treasurer—at that time a director—calling the general manager and not getting any follow-up. That was two and a half years ago. I then remember hearing something about their Southern California office. This is the main office for the marina master lease holder. There was something about an investigation of monies missing. There was another discussion about our relationship with the general manager being a bit shaky due to personalities with past commodores. I did remember that the owner came to our opening day the year before so we should be good there. It seemed to fall back on the general manager. I was just about finished with my mindless job when it dawned on me. I had heard last year that our marina folks had found their problem. *Boom*—I had a brain fart—that's it! I got online and started looking around. I was looking for my secret weapon, and I found it.

Now I needed a proposal in writing so it could not be misinterpreted by the representative. He seemed like a nice guy, but this was my baby. I would not be delivering it in person. The next best thing was to submit it in black and white and see what happened. And for peace of mind, since I could not tell anyone about this, I called a lawyer I had seen about a property question some years back. He was still in practice. I wanted a professional opinion on this proposal I had. I was able to make an appointment the next day.

I sat down and drafted up my thoughts so they were now in front of me. I could now make a proper pitch for resolution of the catch-up fees and open the door for the lease extension without jeopardizing this deal and pissing him off.

I gathered up all the material I had on this matter, along with the proposed resolution. My appointment was at 1:00 p.m. He remembered me and knew that I was still in the area and horsing around. He also was a horseman that enjoyed his animals. I told him what was going on. I explained to him all the details and that I had documents he might want to see. I stated, "I just want you to review this with me and at the end give your honest opinion. Am I crazy, or if you were the judge mediating this, would you feel this was a fair offer with facts that I have presented?" He read my page-and-a-half proposal. He said my offer seemed negotiable considering the circumstances. He wished me luck. I thanked him and drove home. I e-mailed the representative and said, "You will be receiving my proposal in one hour via e-mail. I need to make up the attachment. Remember I am only putting this on the table because of your request for urgency." No matter, the board had to make the final decision. I sent the e-mail Thursday afternoon, on March 12. He said, "Thank you. I will contact you the beginning of next week."

I was not nervous but relieved that this was done. Whatever happened from here would be what it would be. The next day was Friday the thirteenth and the birthday bash. I was praying my luck would be good. The next evening was the Saint Patrick's Day dinner. It was well attended, and everyone loved the young Irish dancers.

I went back and stayed with Sally. She was doing OK. Her sixty-first birthday was just a month away, and she had every intention to make that date. She was not ready to go yet. She commended me for my bravery on submitting the proposal. I appreciated that because she and the people receiving it were the only ones involved. Where we went from here would be interesting. I asked, "Would like to read it?"

She said, "I would rather you read it to me. I would really like that. I like hearing your voice. You tell such interesting stories." Sally would always say, "Tell me a story." We had only been together for four years.

It was addressed to the owner.

Dear sir,

As the incoming commodore for this year, it is my responsibility to secure our new lease with you. A reasonable agreement on the back fees over the past ten years needs to be reached. It would have been much easier to have paid the increase as it accumulated per year than to receive a full sum at the end of a ten-year period showing as delinquent when it was not appropriately applied due to lack of management. It was not our responsibility to calculate and apply it to our rent. We paid our invoices as stated. The cam fees were not on the invoice either. In mid 2012, it was realized by us that we had not been charged nor paid the cam charges. Your main office was notified, and payment started at that time. There was no follow-up by your office after the phone conversation between our director and your general manager.

My duties as commodore also include, once our lease is extended, to get this facility in compliance with the state and local agencies with a handicap lift. That expense is estimated at $26,000, not including permits and architectural engineered drawings. We at present have been given a temporary waiver with the understanding we are moving forward. We had a potential fine of a $2,500 imposed by the state for the problem. We have lost a few members because we could not accommodate their need to access the club.

Another issue that is of great importance is the waste water lines. The bar floor sink continually backs up causing flooding in the bar area which leaks into our office below. The floor drain in our lower kitchen needs major repair. That estimate is around $6,000 because the pipe is in the concrete slab. The floor tile and slab need to be cut in order for it to be replaced. Both of these issues threaten our ability to make money to support our club. If the health department was aware of these problems, they would shut us down until repaired. We can not repair these problems without a lease.

With those burdens, the outstanding rent and cam fees and in good faith for our future relationship, I would request a payment schedule over a five-year period to resolve this.

A meeting was set with your representative on the twenty-seventh of February. It was discussed that the CPI increase on the security deposit be dropped and remain at $8,000. The cam fees should be paid $16,600 for 2005 until mid 2012. When asked about the CPI rent increase, which had not been applied over the ten-year period, I replied, "Let's split it." The total is $27,740, making our share $13,870. Our rent increase in the new lease would be around $2,100, plus the cam fee. We are currently paying $1,700 plus cam fee of $200. This is an increase of $400 per month plus cam fees.

Here is my proposal:

Rent	$13,870
Cam	$16,600
Total	$30,470
Elect	-4,961
Total	$25,509

60 payments at $425 = $25,500

I would be putting this on the table. Our board meeting is Tuesday, the seventeenth of March.

I made an appointment with a real estate lawyer up here in my area which is Santa Ynez. I gave his name and number. I just wanted to put this on the table with an unopinionated professional. I explained the complete situation, including your past general manager's legal problems and his inability to do the job he was hired for, to look out for your investments, not his. I offered the above as a honorable solution. We do not need lawyers. He thought my offer was reasonable considering all circumstances. It was his opinion if this would go to mediation, it would be fair to both parties.

Knowing the members on the board, I believe they will want to low ball using the four-year statues. That has been their thinking. I will try moving my proposed offer forward if you would give me your blessings. I might still have to bring you their decision first before I push this. I will have to read the mood of the meeting, before I make a move.

We certainly have the cart before the horse, but I believe with my thirty-five years as a horseman, I can get the horse in front of this cart. We do not want to involve the Harbor Commission or the County. So let's try to make a deal. This is only being presented because of its urgency.

Respectfully submitted,
The Commodore

CHAPTER 19

I T WAS BECOMING APPARENT THAT Sally was going to have to commit to having her place set up for hospice. She needed someone available close by. She lived in a nice location, which had a vineyard. There was a cutting horse facility within view from her window on the second floor.

This was her living space. There was a guest bedroom. At first, the caregiver used that space. Sally decided that was too close. There was a downstairs room used for entertaining that now became a space for the caregivers to stay. This provided privacy for everyone. This made life a little better until she needed more assistance. That would soon be in the near future.

It was now Monday, the sixteenth of March. I stayed quite busy that day. Another mind-provoking job was mowing pasture on a tractor with a bush hog mower. I referred to this task as tractor time. Once you engaged in this tedious job, you could then find your Zen, while still doing something that takes time. Besides, who is going to bother you? Now busy mowing in the middle of a big pasture.

You cannot hear the phone, and now you are in the zone. At this point, you can solve or create whatever in your head. Just don't forget to turn at the corners and look back to see what might be happening behind you once in a while. Don't forget the sunscreen because it's going to be a while.

After several hours of mowing, it was time to check into reality. There had been no calls. I went and checked the computer for any updates. There were none that I was interested in. It was time to feed and check the horses. After finishing those chores, it seemed like a good day to hit happy hour at the local watering hole. It was that time of the day. Unlike my boat's sign, which read "It's Five O'clock Somewhere!" I was hoping to hear the results of my proposed resolution. The meeting was Saturday, so something must have happened.

It was time to mosey home and see if there might be a reply to my question. I went to the computer, and there was a reply. It read that he accepted my offer on one condition: I pay this off in two and a half years instead of five. "Let me know." That was music to my years. I was going to be more aggressive in my offer to propose a two-and-a-half-year payback, but I thought it better to ask for more, offering a negotiating field. Wow, what a feeling. Of course, I replied immediately.

"Yes, I accept these terms. Now I need board approval. Thank you very much for this opportunity. I will get back to you on Wednesday morning after the meeting. Thanks again!"

I shared this with Sally. She was very happy for me. It would have been nice to celebrate this moment with her, but we were living life and she was struggling with it. We just chilled and had a quiet evening.

It was time to start thinking of how to approach this with the board. I did not want them to think I was undermining them. That could become a problem. Once again it was time to start the morning as a high-fiber engineer and then switch to an executive officer with a proposal in hand.

It was the seventeenth of March, which was Saint Patrick's Day. I was not Irish, but I would take all the lucky charms I could get! This was going to be an interesting evening. If anybody had a better idea, great like cash in hand. This position on the board was voluntary for there were no perks, just the reality of your efforts. A brokered deal with $15,533 savings and two-and-a-half-year monthly payback period and no interest on $25,500—that was $41,200. I thought that was going be hard to beat, but you cannot count your chickens before they hatch.

It was time for the meeting, and everyone was in attendance. We did our usual business. There was really nothing other than get in the closed session and get this discussion going. After the regular meeting it was decided to call a five-minute recess. No one but the board was there. It seemed the right thing to do. I had not shared anything with anyone before our meeting. Going in cold turkey made them a little nervous and figuring this could be a long night. I thought the best approach was to write my proposed figures on a scratch pad and explain in detail my thought process. It seemed a more genuine approach like we were working together on this. I tore that page out of my pad and gave it to the treasurer and asked if she would go downstairs and make ten copies during the recess. She returned with the copies, and I called the meeting to order. I started out by saying we could start discussing how to deal with this catch-up-fee thing we had with our landlord. It was important to keep in mind that what we did would affect our negotiations for the lease extension for the next ten years. "I would like to make a suggestion on how that might be done before opening the floor." No one challenged me. I said I had put a lot of thought since the discovery of this issue. The treasurer and I had an off-site meeting with their representative on the twenty-seventh of February. Its intent was not to make a deal but more on what we might understand on what they're thinking. What was said was they were willing to drop the CPI on the security deposit, which is $1,663. The question of the cam fees of $16,600 was asked. I said we should pay the full amount. These were expenses out of your pocket because you have to pay the cam fees for the master lease. Ours was a kick in the bucket in comparison to the amount cam fees you pay for the master lease. The next question was we owed $27,740 due to the CPI increase over the past ten years on our rent. I said I think we should split that. Had the CPI been applied to the monthly rent over the past ten years, this would not have happened. We paid the amount that was on our statement each month and we discovered the cam fees in mid 2012 and started paying them then. The main office was notified, but no action was taken. I said to the representative that I was giving him my opinion. Anything we did had to be board approved. He decided he had heard enough and thanked us for meeting with him.

So I asked the treasurer to pass out those copies to each director and one for the secretary's file. Now everyone had that paper in hand and I reviewed what I was saying earlier. The math as they saw it was self-explanatory in my mind. I said, "If you were to agree to what I am suggesting, I would also request a payback period of five years to be paid monthly in our rent schedule." Well, it appeared I had their attention. There were a few questions, but it was more like they just wanted to say something. I was looking for something bigger. One of the directors asked to speak. I said yes. "I just want to say I have been in the real estate business for forty-one years. They could say we owe all of this and not make a deal. What I will say is if you can pull this one off, you're our golden boy." Now that was what I was looking for. This gentlemen was eighty-nine years old and our senior past commodore of 1977.

I think I just got the board on board with this deal. There was a motion to accept my proposal and move forward with it. There was a second, no comment. It was unanimously accepted. I asked for copies to be returned and reiterated that this was not to be discussed with anyone. There was no more business. We moved back into the open session and adjourned the meeting. The closed session was less than twenty minutes. You know I drove home with a grin on my face.

It was a pleasant drive home. It was nice getting home by ten o'clock. The year before, you would be lucky to arrive at eleven o'clock. It seemed like a good night to sit on the porch with a glass of Irish whiskey and a fine cigar. I toasted to my lucky stars in the night sky and felt pretty blessed at the same time. Cheers to the night. I would be sharing my news in the morning with Sally.

It was a new day with a purpose in mind. The morning rounds needed to be made, making sure the horses were standing on four legs and eating. When your morning starts, you have a plan, but that can change very quickly around here. With livestock and acreage come a lot of responsibility. It just so happened all was well in my world. I was thinking about the best approach to seal this deal, since I knew what the bottom line was I just had to get the board to seal this deal. I decided to start calling directors at 10:00 a.m. I would tell them I sent our proposal in last night via e-mail. I received confirmation of its arrival. I then received a reply that they would accept the proposal with one exception. The catch-up fees of $25,500 had to be paid in two and one half years instead of five. I thanked them and said I would contact the directors for their approval. As soon as I had five directors' approval, I would send an e-mail out requesting they show approval and I would then forward this to their office. Their reply was, "Great, we are waiting!"

I called the director who made his challenge to me to get this done. He picked up and I told him their offer. He said, "You have my approval." I explained to him my plan of the e-mail approving this deal. I was hoping to have that out to the board by 12:00 p.m. for their approvals via e-mail to be forwarded to the main office. He said, "I will turn my computer on now and be ready." I thanked him and called another director. I explained the offer and again had his approval and explaining the e-mail vote. Next director, same reaction, approved. Fourth director, wrong number, it was his wife. Their cell numbers were the opposite of what was in our roster. She relayed my message to him and said, "I will have him call you right away." Number five was the vice commodore, and he answered.

I explained the deal—that they would accept our offer with one change to be paid in two and a half years. There was a hesitation in his voice. "Uh, maybe we should say three years."

I said, "Are you shitting me? That would be like a slap in the face. I have four votes approving this with no question asked."

That was including mine. I needed one more vote for a majority and again more hesitation. Then I was getting another call. He said, "I won't get in your way, I will give you my vote later." I disconnected him for the other caller. This was the director calling back. I explained to him the deal and the e-mail approval process. He was in. This was my fifth and final needed to construct that e-mail for their approval. Once out, it was taking a while for the approvals. I once again called each director and asked them to respond as soon as possible. I did not want to have to deal with this any longer. It was done and now needed board confirmation. After I received their approval, this was forwarded to the main office as well to the representative directly. I called and told him I was done and to please confirm by e-mail. There were two directors I did not bother calling. Even if they would have approved, their conversations would have been grueling. The e-mail was forwarded around 2:00 p.m. I received confirmation from the representative that this was accepted and approved on their end at 4:00 p.m. I then e-mailed the approval that a job was well done. "Thank you." I did receive a reply of his approval at 10:00 p.m. from the vice commodore. *Gee, thanks*, I thought to myself.

You would think I could put my feet up and relax, but that was not in the cards. Thursday, I was the guest speaker at our in-house women's cooking group. It is customary that the incoming commodore speak at this dinner sharing your life story. Giving some insight to how you got here.

You pay for your own meal, eat, and then entertain this group for thirty minutes or so. The board members are asked to attend along with anyone else who might be interested. After what I have just gone through and now being asked to give my personal story was a challenge in itself.

When I was done, I did receive a round of applause. I guess you might say I did good.

The next day was the general meeting. I was sharing our good fortune with our making a deal on the catch-up fees with a past commodore. He then said I would need to get the members' approval because it was an expenditure over $1,500. You can imagine how fun that might be.

CHAPTER 20

OUR MEETINGS IN THE PAST have been referred to as those of a homeowner's association meeting. That is why the attendance is not always as good as one would like. I said, "Thanks for the good news." I put it on the agenda. I believed this would really have gone before a special meeting, so I really had to hold my own, and if I got approval, I would notify the membership via e-mail in the morning in case I got challenged. There was no time to pussyfoot around now.

It was now time to call this meeting to order. We had a quorum. We did the Pledge of Allegiance to our flag. I had asked the chaplain to pray for a miracle while doing the invocation. The meeting continued without much interference. It was now time for the commodore's agenda.

Very few people had been aware of any catch fees and those that did have said nothing. So I was starting again cold turkey. I stated that there was something preventing us from making a smooth transition into the ten-year lease extension. After some calculation at the request of our landlord, it had been determined that we were in default on our commitment in the past ten years. In order to move forward, this needed to be resolved. I received this notice and the estimated figure that was arrived at. I had a closed session meeting with the board at our February meeting to this and the amount we were in debt. Now you can imagine the facial expression in the audience. I believe I was interrupted, some asking, "Well, how much? How did this happen?"

I said, "I am getting to that. I have the floor and there will be no more interruption until I am done. And it will be one person at a time, at my approval." I returned to my thought process. I had notes, but I did not need them. This helped keep everyone engaged with me. I said there was a meeting with their representative off-site. These matters were discussed only for understanding, not to make any final offer. We had our board meeting this last Tuesday evening. We did have a closed session and reviewed this. I explained what had been discussed at our meeting with their representative. I disclosed my train of thought on the matter. I had been thinking of the way to resolve these catch-up fees in a manner best for the club as well as maintaining an open forum with the landlord so as not to jeopardize moving forward with our lease extension that would end this June 30, 2015.

So let me share with you what the board has decided with the best interest for the future our yacht club. The total of the catch-up fees over the past ten years was $46,161. The crowd was going to explode. I said there was much more to explain before the floor would open for discussion. Thank you. Now we had one deduction to bring this down a little. We overpaid our electric bill by $4,961. This brought their figure to $41,200. Let me explain the breakdown on that. The cost of living increase over the past ten years had not been applied. So with that being said, the CPI on the security deposit is $1,633. The CPI on our monthly rent is $27,740. There was a monthly charge common area, which was $200 a month. This total was $16,600. It was discovered in mid 2012 that we had not been paying but started paying the $200 per month and that had been credited to our account. There was a short discussion with their representative. It was disclosed they would drop the $1,663 on the security deposit. When asked about the cam fees, I said I felt they should be paid. They were paid monthly in the master lease, but they were not reimbursed for them, so that was $16,600. I was asked about the rent of $27,740. I said we should split it. That would be $13,870 each. After that, their representative had heard enough, and our meeting was at an end. If this proposal were accepted, our debt would be $25,500. Actually it was $25,509 if anybody was doing the math. I would pay the nine bucks just to make it even. This was a deduction of $15,533 from the original $41,200. I presented this to the board along with a possible payment plan. We would be asking that if they would accept this proposal. We also requested a five-year payment plan to be paid with our rent payment. After a little discussion and positive feedback, the board approved this proposal be offered as a solution to our debt and open the door for our ten-year lease agreement. I gave this proposal to our landlord at their request for a solution to the catch-up fees. This agreement was accepted with one change: that we pay this in two and a half years, not five. The majority of the board agreed to these terms. "I would be asking you to support your board on their decision on this matter."

Well, you can imagine watching the roller coaster ride on these people's faces. Now it was time to get their opinion. What are you going to say to someone who spelled it all out in plain English? They got a little emotional about how this happened. "It was not our fault, they screwed up."

I called the meeting point of order. "If you think there is a better solution, say it." No further complaining. "Does someone have an objective comment?" Order was kept, and they did accept this resolution, and our lease would be now in the process of going forward. One comment about the meeting was there were eight staff commodores at the meeting. Each raised their hand to take a turn to speak. They all raised concern on the problem. What all stated in their own words was that the solution presented this evening in their opinions was a just and fair solution for both sides. The second to the last commodore to speak recommended we take use our savings account and pay this debt in full. The reaction to that was why we would deplete our savings when this can be paid back over two and a half years with no interest? He sat down. One other member asked to speak. He too was not happy we had gotten behind but felt the solution should be approved. This member can be very opinionated and was a bit combative in my first meeting, but this meant a lot to me. After the last meeting in January, I received a bag from someone with a note. It was from this member. There was a gavel in it, and the note said, "I apologize for my directness at the meeting the other night. I realized you did not have a gavel. I understood it had been taken. So here is your gavel, and I downloaded a few copies of the Robert Rules of Order. I thank you for stepping up, and I myself would not want to do it. Thank you." The last commodore to speak was my board member who said he believed a round of applause should be given for a job well done and something about my ability to walk on water. We did get the applause.

It would now be very important to craft and e-mail to the membership, stating all of last night's business and the final outcome. I had it e-mailed the first thing in the morning. It was important we were all on the same page, so there was no room for dissent on this matter. We were now on our way to lease and a bright future for our club. There were no replies.

As soon as the agreement and lease were signed, I could call for a special meeting of the membership to address the chairlift.

The meeting was on March 20, and I would hope to have the lease in hand for an announcement on opening day, April 12. That did not happen, but it was in the process.

What did happen was our office was asked to draft up our agreement on the catch-up fees. We now had both the board and membership approval. That would not be a problem. It was a Wednesday. I requested the treasurer to make two originals to be delivered to their main office. I would be down later to sign both documents. I would arrive so they could be sent overnight by courier mail to arrive the next day. The second original could be signed by them and sent back by regular mail, but they could e-mail a copy to our office in the meantime. This sounded good to me. I was on my way when their representative called and asked the treasurer to send him a copy before the originals be sent to the main office. I was informed upon my arrival of his request. I said, "I cannot imagine what that is about. This is already in black and white. Send him a copy, and we will still send these to the main office." I signed the agreements and overnighted them. Done deal!

CHAPTER 21

THE FOLLOWING WEEK, THE OFFICE received his revised agreement. It stated that the catch-up fees were now to be paid back in two years, not two and a half as originally agreed upon. Well, this did not settle with me at all. How can this be? I remembered in the conversation with the treasurer on the way home from our first meeting with this guy she mentioned she had reservations about him. It was in reference to his talking about his background he shared as a real estate developer. She said, "I am a lawyer, and you know the joke about how lawyers should be weighted down and dropped to the bottom of the ocean—well, I think that about most realtors."

I was not going to humor this guy with an e-mail or phone call. I was going around him. I had the owner's personal e-mail, and I was going straight to the top for an answer on this matter. It read,

> Dear sir,
>
> I was asked by your representative to send a proposal describing our conversation on February 27 about the catch-up fees. When asked to present you my thoughts on a resolution on March 12, I did. I told him I should not do this, but he stated you were going to South America and would be gone for two weeks, so I sent it to him for your review. I received an e-mail from him on March 16.
>
> It stated that you would agree but with a two and half year pay-off. On March 17, I pre-

sented this to the board with this agreement but stated the original proposal of five years. You and I had already had this discussion via your representative before that meeting. After that meeting, I called each board member the following morning stating that you accepted the proposal but it should be paid in two and half years. I put out an e-mail so they could approve this providing you proof of acceptance so we could move forward with the lease extension. That was forwarded to your office on March 18.

March 30, your representative asked our treasurer to draft up our agreement and have me sign it. I told him it was done and I would be signing it April 2 and to send it on April 2. He then requested a copy be e-mailed to him. He then told the treasurer he had some questions about it and would get back to her. We sent the document to your main office. Today being April 6, at 3:13 p.m., the office received his e-mail, stating the $25,500 was to be paid in two years. If you have any questions, call and he will get back to her with any comments from your attorney.

Now what was sent to your office was exactly what we supposedly agreed to. It was approved by our board on March 18, the membership March 20, and an e-mail sent out to the full membership so there would be no gossip, only fact. It is April 6, and now there is a game change. Our opening day is Sunday. I was hoping this would be done by then.

We will accept the change in the game plan. I just do not appreciate being blindsided. No need to respond. I just wanted to state the facts.

The Commodore

The next morning, I received a call from the treasurer. She received a message from the representative that he had made a mistake in his draft changes and that our original was correct.

I told her what I had done, sending an e-mail to the owner expressing my thoughts on this matter. I forwarded her a copy for her eyes only.

Her reply, "Yes, I think he had a little help in changing his tune and played it our way."

I said, "You were right in your evaluation of him."

The documents we had sent to the office were now lost, so we were asked again to send them with my signature. This time, they were sent regular mail.

The representative stayed involved even after this deal was brokered, and the lease was to be signed by all parties. He was getting on my nerves. Every time he e-mailed, he would ask, "Where are you with the permit process with your chairlift?" I would say as I had before, I needed a signed lease. A special meeting with the membership on their approval on both the unit as well as the money needed to fund this program. But he just kept inquiring, so I finally ignored the man. I would let him know when that time came.

From that point, I addressed everything with the local office. I asked them to be the middle person. I had no problem keeping them informed. In fact, they were very helpful and supportive. That kind of relationship could get things done. Since it appeared that this was going to be a waiting game, it was time to check in the vertical platform lift cost. We had an individual chairlift mounted on our back patio stair railing. It had been installed in February of 2012. It was always breaking down and was not reliable. It was found not be in compliance in 2014. It was to be removed by a chairlift licensed contractor. The company this unit was purchased from had just been bought out by a new company. This actually worked in our favor. When the new owner came out to check our unit, he offered a $4,000 discount on our unit and free removal of that unit if we would buy our new unit from them. The new vertical platform lift was around $26,000. That made our price $22,000 with the discount. I assumed that when pitching this to the membership that it could be a price point. Similar units were in the $26,000 range or more. So I had that information. I had called the city inspector about the permit process. I was told our relationship might be a bit shaky from prior occasions. I called and left a message, introducing myself as the new commodore, and said I was inquiring about a permit for a vertical platform lift to be installed in our back patio area. "If you could please give me a call and let me know what that might entail, I would appreciate your input. Thanks." The building inspectors were in the field a lot. I received a call from him a few days later. He gave me the information I was seeking, so when the time came we were all on the same page. He would be the one looking at the architectural engineer's drawings. The electrical was already there because of the other unit. I got bids from four architectural engineer firms. They were $3,800 to $7,000. After checking, the electrical was found to be underwired. This meant the existing wiring was no. 12.

Our unit needed no. 10 wiring. The conduit was already there. The unit once in place would have to be hardwired into the 30-amp breaker box. Two motion detector floods were to be added for night light.

Not a lot to do. The bids for the electrical were $3,000 to $6,000. I would just shake my head. As a rancher and past handyman, I thought I was in the wrong business. Well, I persevered and found a local electrical contractor who would work with us, and his bid was $1,500. I had all that done now. How were we going to pay for this? Our bank would give us a line of credit. And we would use our savings account as collateral. I spoke to a commercial equipment lease company. The company we were looking at buying the unit from had no financing. We at one time or so, I have been told, had $25,000 in an elevator fund. That would show on the books, but there was around $750 in the account. The other money was used over the years to fund other projects. Of course, we would start another donation drive and this time with a special bank account. Once this project was to get started, we could not stop. It was all or nothing.

I was finally contacted that our lease extension was signed by the owner who held the master lease. The next signature that was needed was the harbor master. It was now April 21 and time for our board meeting. After our usual meeting it was time for me to address the board on the chairlift for our club. I explained I had the bids and understood the permitting process. I felt we would be ready to address the membership. I was about to explain all this to them when our senior past commodore, now director, stated that we didn't need to hear this. "You need to sell the membership."

At that point, I said, "I am ready to address the membership at a special meeting." I directed the secretary to draft up that notice. The date of the meeting would be Friday, May 8. This needed to be mailed tomorrow. That would keep us in the guideline of the two-week notice by mail. This would be a seventeen-day period. The letter was drafted, approved, and mailed the following day.

What was happening before this were all the preparations for opening day. Several ship-shapes later, as they are referred to, was our opening day celebration. As commodore, it is customary to attend most other yacht clubs' opening day ceremonies. There were four on the Saturday and three on Sunday, including ours. There is an association for the Santa Barbara Channel Yacht Clubs. These events are set at different times so you could attend them all. I had a great staff that made sure that ours was an outstanding event. The food was prepared by our in-house cooking groups. The club had been decorated and looked quite festive. The opening day in our harbor started with a boat parade with all clubs participating with members and their club officers aboard. The air was filled with cannon fire celebrating the opening day as we passed each yacht club. We all took a moment to acknowledge those who crossed over with the ringing of the eight bells and the bagpipes playing "Amazing Grace." It was truly a celebration of life with the sea. At the end of each one's ceremony, the commodore asked the port captain, "Is the harbor free of ice?"

Usually it is the commodore who calls "fire in the hole." The cannoneer fired the cannon one more time for the end of the opening day ceremony. Now it was time to eat and drink and share our facilities.

Another thing that happened was last year's commodore had to make a scene. He sent out an e-mail stating that the office had lost his checks totaling $750 and stating that the audit committee should be reenacted. This did not make me very happy. I knew he was wrong, but we had to chase the paper trail. I had my friend drive down and follow up on this matter along with the treasurer. Sure enough, he was wrong again. This was the Friday before our board meeting. How convenient it was that he was unable to attend our board meeting to have this explained to him.

Instead it was explained to the vice commodore, because technically he was the CFO but was not really doing that job. So he could officially do something in that capacity with us providing the information. Of course, when the past commodore realized that he had made the mistake, he e-mailed and said that he appreciated the vice commodore finding this and corrected his mistake. He went on to say that we all make mistakes.

I knew better than that, and I sent him a letter expressing his insulting manner of getting an answer to a question. He made it more of a threat than just a mistake. He should consider apologizing to the office staff for his blunder. I also took the time to make up another complaint against him in case he thought I was just blowing smoke. I just said, "Keep this type of misconduct up and this will become official. By the way, it appears you did not pay your last quarter dues for 2014. We had to write off close to three thousand dollars in delinquent dues or ones that were incorrectly recorded. I am sorry if you are stating that we lost checks that you can prove you paid. How about showing me a stub from the one you wrote and we have no record of receiving one." There were a couple of other things I discovered and notified him as well. He did bring a new check to the May board meeting for his dues. It was marked as a replacement check. There was no proof he had ever paid them. The only reason this came about was his threat to the office, so I looked very close at all of his activities. He who called wolf got bit.

At this point, Sally was now in full hospice. I came in one afternoon, and the caregiver was downstairs. When I walked up the stairs, in the middle of the room was a bucket with a mop in it. Sally liked a clean house. I went into the bedroom, and Sally was asleep on the bed with the TV on. I quietly lay on the bed next to her. I did not want to wake her. A little while later, she woke and realized I was there. She gave me a smile and then got a serious look on her face. She said, "I need to finish mopping the floor."

I said, "Honey, just let it go, that is not your job anymore." Her birthday was just few days away. For her birthday, I got a large vase of beautiful flowers. She could see them and they were specifically picked for their fragrances. It was important to me for them to last as long as possible. Every time I came over, all she could talk about were smells she was enjoying and waking up to each day.

We finally received a copy of a signed lease. I was not pressuring our local office, but I would express the clock was running. I was the commodore for one year, and it was almost May. I wanted to do what I could while in office. I believed with our ability to work together, we could succeed at whatever we want. They were certainly on board with that.

Well, the only thing left to do now in regards to the lift was to wait for Friday, May 8, and present this to the membership.

May was looking pretty quiet as far as the calendar. We were all recuperating from April's events. As commodore, I was still attending the opening days for the other yacht clubs in Southern California. Our bocce ball season would start this month on the second Thursday and going until October. Always a well-attended and fun time.

We would have a cruise weekend over the Memorial Day holiday to the islands and return to the club for our holiday supper club on Monday afternoon. There was a sailboat race the last weekend.

Sally was slowly fading away. Each day was a little more difficult, so her doses were adjusted for the pain. She continued hanging on. I was having a hard time with this. Her family was taking turns staying with her. They all lived in the Los Angeles Area. Her best friend, as she referred to him, was her ninety-five-year-old father. He was quite healthy and still lived at home with a little assistance. The last time I was at Sally's, I left thinking we were more humane to our livestock than people are. I ran a retirement facility. Horses came to me to be turned out on grass pasture and live their days out with their buddies. Some of them lived as long as ten to fifteen years in retirement. My requirements were if you lay down, you needed to able to get up, and what goes in, meaning hay, comes out. Those were pretty simple terms. When those requirements were not met, it was then time to evaluate the situation. For me, it is very sad when a horse is taken away just to die elsewhere, when all they wanted is a good life with a great memory of where they found that space. This may sound a little harsh, but when you are no longer in control anymore, what?

I received a call that Sally had passed. It just so happened that it was Cinco de Mayo, May 5. Sally's favorite drink was a margarita. She could make a good one, but we enjoyed one at our favorite place for happy hour, and they did make a good one for the price. So this was a good date to remember, and always cheers to Sally, and I thanked her for the time we were able to share.

So now it was May 8, the day of the meeting. Was I ready to do this? Yes. Did I feel like I could do this today maybe? I would rather not, but this meeting was planned over two weeks ago, and life went on.

As a former member of the United States Marine Corps and a Vietnam veteran, if you had just lost your comrade—this time it was my lady—it was time to lock and load. We were not put on this earth to let them down. You had to stand up and move on. It was who we are. You grabbed yourself by the bootstraps and stayed engaged.

All the figures were embedded in my head. I did not need notes. Mentally, it just seemed trying to make my points. The meeting was called to order. It was not important that they be aware that Sally had passed. It was, "Are you interested in a commitment to this project." I had researched this effort that went on since 1977. This was the beginning of my presentation for their approval of this project. Our building was renovated with the improvement of an elevator in 1977. The electrical and footing for the hydraulic piston and the enclosure were built within this remodel.

Ten thousand dollars had been donated by one individual for the purchase of the elevator. In that day, this was built within the building and the elevator would support four to five people. The commodore at the time was not able to succeed during his term, so the following year, the project was scrapped and the money put in the general fund. In those days, there were no requirements. It was stated by the next commodore if you could not enter by the stairway after the second attempt, you would not qualify as a member. Well, this got their attention. Now I explained how this could happen and made comparisons to other units and offered the offer extended to us with our last investment to resolve our issue. I explained the price comparison that was offered to us as a valid discount compared to other units. I suggested the extended warranty because we lived in an area of difficult weather conditions. I felt at the end of two years, we should be able see how this unit held up in our sea conditions. Salt erosion is a big deal. It was stated to us that their process would alleviate those issues. As I was getting more engaged in the explanation it was apparent this could be difficult to sell. The expressions on the people's faces were unbelievable. Our membership was a mixture of people who remembered the depression to those that knew the reality of progress.

CHAPTER 22

ONCE THE OPEN DISCUSSION STARTED, I disengaged. If this was not going to be resolved tonight, it would never be on my agenda the rest of the year. I was mentally exhausted and had nothing further to say. The parliamentarian and a few other past commodores realized we were this close to doing this and handling that detail. Once the meeting was in order, proper motions were made. "Do you want to have a vertical platform installed?" "Do you want to give the commodore the authority to fund this with the options he has offered?" First off, the purchase and installation were approved, and then the bank line credit was called for a vote and was approved. The subject of donation was also discussed. I did receive some members' concerns that this had been done before without the results it was intended for.

All I could say was that was then and this was now. When this was happening, I believe it was understood if you did not approve of what I was presenting you tonight, it would not be on my agenda again this year. I also provided a completion date, which was to be before our disabled veterans sailed, an event on July 26. With that being said, I hoped that it would be understood I was serious. "So let's get on the bandwagon and get it done." I was relieved to have this behind me and now to focus forward.

After the meeting was adjourned, a member came up to the podium and said, "I am writing you a check for ten thousand dollars, and if you need the line of credit, let me know." I received a total $12,800 at the end of the meeting. That felt pretty damn good. When I went into the bar, people were very pleased that this had been accomplished. Now I needed to deliver. Some people were discussing how we might make money to support this project. Two ladies were discussing the auctioning of our bachelors and looking at me as one of the candidates. I said sorry, I would be too busy with this project.

Mother's Day luncheon was the tenth of May, and the board of directors were responsible for the preparing and serving the food. It was a nice dinner, and a rose was presented to each mother, along with complimentary champagne.

When I returned home after the Mother's Day luncheon, I sat down and put together an e-mail to the membership explaining the results of the special meeting. I found it best to inform our members on important issues so we were all on the same page.

> At the beginning of the presentation, I offered a little history on the elevator saga. A lot of folks were unaware that in 1977, our club house was being renovated. There was an elevator shaft constructed, the footing for the elevator poured, and the electricity was installed. The money to purchase the elevator had been donated by Captain A. A. Oakley. At that time, our most senior past commodore was at the helm. He was unable to complete this effort with in his year as commodore. The incoming commodore decided that the elevator was not needed and stopped the project. Over the years, there have been several attempts to do something, but all were lost in some transition. It is now 2015, and thirty-eight years later, this will be done in time for our Disabled Veterans Sail Day event on July 26.
>
> Thank you.
> The Commodore

It was now time to implement my plan. I drove to Ventura and spoke to the architectural engineer firm and signed a contract to get them rolling on our project. After that, it was time to talk with the marina office and lay out my plan to get this done. When researching the permit process online, I found a construction permit application and printed it out. I was going to request that the marina owners who had the master lease apply as the property owner. They would be responsible and liable for the construction. It was their building and they had their own crew for whatever was necessary. Realistically, all they had to do was cut the railing where this self-standing unit attached to the second-floor walkway. The vertical platform lift was to be installed by the company we were purchasing from. They were their own contractor, and the only other thing was the electrician, who was his own contractor. We just paid the fees for the permit, and I would be the trail boss, making sure all went as planned. I put a package together and sat down in their office and explained my proposal. They were on board with this. I said I would propose this to the owner, and when asked, they had all the details to help this along. It was agreed they would support my proposal as long as I could sell it to their boss. In past attempts, something would trip up the process and kill it. This time, I had a formula that should not fail.

I returned home and typed up an e-mail to the owner with my proposal. I realized this approach might seem a little unorthodox, but shoot me for trying. As I have stated before, we had never met, but we had been dealing the cards pretty well up to this time. I did start my request with an apology.

Dear sir,

I apologize for knocking on the front door, but I would like to reach out once again for your support. I explained in great detail what I was asking for and how this would all be accomplished. I stated that the permit application that needs his signature and structural design and installation information provided by the manufacturer were given to your office for review.

I included those attachments along with the e-mail. This was done on Thursday morning. I drove down to the local office and asked if they heard anything about my request. I wanted to be there personally this was to important to call and inquire about. Later that day, they did receive a call from the owner about my request. He seemed to accept my proposal. His question was, "How much is this going to cost me?" It was stated nothing, the Yacht Club would cover all cost. They just felt this approach would help their process have a little more clout using our name. We were the owners of the building. We were now backed up by the big guns. I just needed his signature on this permit. His signature had to be notarized. All the signatures on the permit had to be notarized. This took close to two weeks, but I finally received it. At that point, I hand-carried and received all necessary signatures.

Once I received the owner's commitment, it was time to bite the bullet. I needed to order the unit.

Two payments needed to be made, which totaled around $15,000. Now that is a commitment. It would take six weeks from the date of signing a contract and this deposit before the unit would arrive at our facility. Do or die—let's do it so now the ball is rolling.

The engineer stated it would take approximately four weeks to have their drawings ready for the city. There was nothing more that could be done until then. Whenever anything was going on, each person involved saw all e-mail communication between us. It was agreed by all parties that this had to be completed by July 26. No excuses.

There were plenty of trials and tribulations during the process. None that were stopping this—just the usual pitfalls in doing a project. This was why I accepted the responsibility as the trail boss. The permit was submitted. A few little details needed to be done. On the second time, it was said it would be approved by the city. It just needed another signature from the harbor district director. This was where he had been stopped before. I was not worried, just had to keep on rolling along.

It was coming time to write my article for our publication. It had to be submitted by the fifteenth of each month. I was in one of my favorite places to write and have breakfast. There was a lot going on in my head. So I just let it all out in the article. I was just being honest with myself and the members.

CHAPTER 23

Howdy, folks, hard to believe it is May already. Here I set writing this to you on my sixty-sixth birthday, feeling healthy and happy and reflecting upon where life has taken me. If you had asked me a year ago what I would be doing now, I would have probably said the same old thing, just another day. Well, that is far from the truth. I persevered through last year then stood back and looked forward. I said, "What do I have to lose?" So I put on my spurs on my boots and saddled up. With your support, we are back in the saddle again. As I stated at the August meeting, there is a new sheriff in town.

I know I am the commodore of your Yacht Club, but life does run in parallel—what does that mean? It means we are in the wind and connected by water, which connects us to everything, making us one with nature. I had nothing to lose by exposing to you who I really am, including my tenacity for life. Obviously I have your attention, so let's have fun and do what is right and get this ship on course.

Our special meeting convinced me that with your support, we will make this Yacht Club one of the premiere examples of what a Yacht Club is supposed to be about. Thank you.

Over the past year, I observed something that I have termed *senior puberty*. I thought as we get older, we become wiser and reflect compassion and wisdom in our lives and move forward.

What I was seeing was the opposite. So I thought I would challenge it and move forward to see who was right. Now that challenge has been answered.

With my recent loss in mind, I leave you with the words that Sally's family texted me: "Sally Jo went home to be with the Lord today. Her spirit is now soaring above us riding free and happy with the wild horses and dogs. Rejoined at last with her loved ones. She was deeply loved and will be truly missed! Ride, Sally, ride! The Giamo Family."

Thank you for your cards, thoughts, and prayers. Just wanted to let you know I am on the mend. Thank you.

Your Commodore

I T WAS NOW THE MONTH of June. We had a British brass concert on the first Tuesday this month. This group had a large following and used our facility to practice at once a month or so. The wet Wednesday sailing had already started and would continue until October when the daylight became shorter. Bocce ball was in full swing. We would be having a special dinner to honor Father's Day.

We hosted our yacht club race to Marina Del Rey the last weekend. The next Sunday was a fun rental by a member. He called it the Song Circle. Musicians were invited to play along with others, which created a great afternoon of entertainment for all. We also had a cruise weekend out to Yellow Banks off Santa Cruz Island.

It seemed the board meetings were staying pretty civilized and short and to the point. All eyes were on the lift progress. The membership was really stepping it up with donation for the project. We had over $24,000 at this time. Once the unit was in our parking lot, another large payment was due. The final amount would be due upon completion, along with a state compliance permit and city inspector's approval. I kept updating the board on these matters.

It was time for our third general meeting of the year. I would be giving a progress report on the chairlift. This was on June 26.

The meeting was going very well. After giving them an update, I was reminding them that our lease of the past ten years was coming to an end on the thirtieth. I wanted to remind them that we would now start paying off our catch-up fee debt, paying monthly for the next two and a half years. Our rent with the cam fees up until now had been $1,900 a month. As of the first of July with the increase in our rent had now been adjusted to the CPI over the past ten years of $418 added to the $1,900. This made the monthly rent $2,318. Our catch-up fee monthly payment was $850. Add the two together—our monthly payment was now $3,168. With this being said, there were some concerned faces in front of me. I had been thinking of this but had not addressed the board. The concern I saw in the audience led me into the no-man zone. I stated we might have to consider a dues increase. Well, that was not how I meant it, but it started a flurry solution by other past commodores. Suddenly, one my directors jumped up and said this was not to be a discussion with the membership. This was board business and we would decide how to go about this. I looked at him straight in the eyes and said, "That's funny, when I approached the board with all the information about the $35,000 for the chairlift, you said you have to sell this to the members, not us." I turned around and said to the members, "I am sorry if I offended anyone. Let's call this a State of the Union address. I am just informing you of some changes you should be aware of." The meeting came to a good end and was adjourned. Some people appreciated my honesty, and others did not. What they thought on this matter would all come out in the laundry.

I did send an e-mail to the complete membership informing them on the meeting the night before. It gave everyone the facts and figures of the chairlift as of that evening. It also included the increase in the rent and the payment of the catch-up fees over the next two and a half years. I boldly went on to say, "We may have to look at ways to deal with these increases." I published a formula that I felt needed to be seen. There again I was stepping out of the box, but this was my box and at least I would be honest about it. There were no replies to this e-mail. I did get a few people who later said they appreciated my honesty and liked the fact that after any important meeting, the membership was informed of what exactly was said.

On July 1, I was feeling like things were going very well and the rest of the year should be a breeze. I had just returned home to find I had received an e-mail at 10:00 p.m. from a past commodore. It said, "If you profess to be the commodore, then act like one." I am sorry, there must have been something in his drink that made him blurb those words out. I decided to not respond but did e-mail his daughter stating, "You might want to have a conversation with your father. I am not going to be back down to the old guard. My concern was, is he up to that task? I am concerned about his ticker (meaning his heart). I just wanted you to know. Thanks. The Commodore."

There was no further ranting on the subject.

As best that I can tell, everything was moving forward with our lift project. The unit was ready and being crated for shipping to our facility. It was scheduled to arrive on Monday, the thirteenth of July. At that point, it would be assembled in the parking lot and hoisted over our wall into the patio area. This put us well within the completion date of July 26.

It was now July, and it was time to celebrate the Fourth of July, Independence Day. There was a big fireworks display for that evening. It was well attended by the community. There was usually no parking space available in the area because of all the people that came to watch the fireworks. For the cruisers, it was a trip out to Coches at Santa Cruz Island. Our annual upcoming event was the last Sunday of the month, which was the disabled veterans' sail day. We offered veterans and their guests the opportunity to go out on the water in a sailboat, powerboat, or just a cruise in the harbor in an electric boat. We provided a light breakfast, and after a three-hour cruise, it was time to feed the masses with tri-tip or chicken and all the sides. The attendance was quite impressive. Stories were shared, and it was just a nice opportunity to honor those who have stepped up to protect and provide us with lives we now share.

I received a call from the office on the afternoon of Monday, July 13. It was reported that our lift had arrived and was in the parking lot. We would need an overnight parking pass. I asked the office if that could be taken care of. We would also be providing security so it would not be tampered with. It was said the crew would be there first thing the next morning to assemble it. I contacted our member who was providing his equipment to lift this unit over the wall and set in place in the patio. All systems were a go.

There were some issues about releasing the building permit. I started working on that as soon as I became aware of it. This was pretty exciting and shutting the naysayers up. This would soon become a reality.

The crew arrived the following day and started assembling our vertical platform lift, which was purchased as completely enclosed self-standing unit that would be bolted in place to our existing slab and brace to the second-story landing. The assembly was going quite fast. This was going to be in place by the end of the day. As it was being lifted over the wall and set on the patio, we were handed our permit. You could say the ink was still wet. That's what you call timing. I was to have the next installment paid that day. It was necessary to call for that loan offered to me. I requested a sum of $10,000 to complete this deal. The loan should be paid back with the next two months. If this were to happen, no interest would be charged. That was a good incentive to work toward. We were right below the budget I had estimated to the members and before schedule of the completion. The crew worked very hard to get this completed by the next day. It was funny—once the unit was in our patio it needed to be tested before placing in its final location. An extension cord was plugged into an electric receptacle and wired to the unit for testing. *All this effort for a self-standing plug-in unit*, I thought to myself. Our unit was now in place and ready for inspection with the city and state compliance certificate.

CHAPTER 24

WE HAD A DINNER PLANNED for Saturday night. It was to be prepared by that men's cooking group, which had imploded back in December. It was stated at the previous board meeting that this would not be done without a meeting with the commodore and the vice commodore. Well, that order was ignored. I knew they had been courting the vice commodore because he was in charge of the dinners. This group had called for a bonding meeting to get their ball rolling. I was going to attend. In fact, I was parked in the parking lot the evening this was to take place. I wanted to hear their pitch. I could not bring myself to enter the building, feeling I was not going to like what I heard. A fellow board member was attending, so I figured I would get the word from him. I turned around and drove back home. What I decided to do was invite myself to the dinner as the guest speaker. I put together an e-mail expressing my desire to take that time and address the members who were in attendance. I called it an evening with the commodore. I sent it out first thing in the morning, and I received the board's approval. I had another e-mail to be released to the membership. This was to be sent out by our communication person. All of a sudden, the man in charge of the dinner, who had been the commodore last year and also a director, said I couldn't do that. An hour before, he had approved this. He had called our communications person and requested a copy of my release to the membership. He had no business doing that. I was the commodore. So this gentlemen called me and said that he was told that he could not send out my release. I informed him, "I am your commodore and I have the majority of the board to back this up. Reword as you may, but this will go out. Are there any further questions?" Time was of the essence. The dinner was in three days, and I wanted it to be sold out. Their original flyer said they were cooking for one hundred. Now they set the cutoff at seventy-five. No matter, it would be a sellout. I explained this was to be a commodore's update and there would be no Q&A. This was strictly an opportunity to have a few moments with the members. I called it an over-the-hump speech. I also said this should be a regular event offering the commodore an opportunity to address the members in a relaxed atmosphere. The only formality would be the bridge officers would have their own tables and invite their guests and people of their choice to join them. This had been customary but had slipped through the cracks.

It was the evening of the dinner. All was going well. No one knew what to expect because this was the first time it had happened. I did have something I wanted to say, but after reading the room, I changed my mind. I started out by thanking all of those who attended. I called a toast to them supporting me in the chairlift endeavor, which was now complete, and also to a new lease on life for the yacht club with the catch-up fees being paid and a new ten-year extension. That was a lot to celebrate. I stated the reason I had decided to do this dinner speech was because I had overheard two ladies saying we should have an auction of our bachelors after the meeting approving the chairlift. "I figured if I got up in front of all of you, we might be able to get a few more donations." There was a donation bucket in the entry. We received another $1,500, and I did not have to sell myself. It was a great evening.

The next Tuesday was our board meeting. I requested the treasurer to e-mail the gentleman who had hand-carried the invoice to the coast guard last year. I wanted him to address the board. Who gave him the authority to deliver that $750 handwritten invoice that was not approved by our office? Our meeting was called to order, and when the time came, I asked the gentleman to answer my question.

He stood up defiantly and said, "I do not have to answer your question. We are a separate entity. I do not have to give you anything."

I asked the director who was on the cooking crew if he had brought their accounting books in with him as I had asked.

He said, "Yes, but I could not look at them unless I was a member."

I said, "The question I have is there were several new apprentices that paid $100 to be in your group. You disbanded, and they were never given their chef coats." This just turned into an exchange of words, which was getting us nowhere. I told the one gentleman who was invited that he could now leave the room.

He asked the judge advocate what my problem was. He was told that I was a former Marine and did not appreciate his insubordinate attitude. We moved on to other business without further incident. I did call for a closed session to address the director's attitude. I was filing the complaint from the April accounting incident. I was asking him to step down from the board. After my presentation to the board, a vote was called for his resignation. Four yes, two nays, one abstained, and one member was absent. A formal letter was sent to this director from the secretary by registered mail. He refused to sign for it. It was later returned to the office. I was awaiting his reply. He was not going to step down as a director. That did not really bother me. I just wanted him to know he would no longer have much to say at our meetings.

CHAPTER 25

I T WAS ONCE AGAIN TIME to pick a nominating committee. The process was to repeat itself. I was to stay on as a director for my remaining year on the board.

Our disabled veterans sail day was a huge success.

It was now August, and our club was involved in helping and supporting our local maritime museum event being hosted by the International Order of the Blue Gavel. This was the first event raising funds for the museum. It was called the Chowder Festival. Local restaurants entered their chowders to be served and judged by the patrons. It was a huge success and gave the museum a good financial boost. We had sailboat races, a dinghy party, and dinners planned in that month. We had a golf tournament that was a memorial tournament in my mentor's honor. The funds raised would go to a junior golfer organization. This was always well attended. The fourth general meeting providing the membership with the next candidates for the next year was the last Friday of the month. All went well. No issues to speak of.

We were now approaching the last quarter of the year. It was now September. This was a fun month of activities. The Wednesday night dinners, birthday bash, a cruise to Fry's over the Labor Day weekend, and returning for the holiday supper club at the Yacht Club. It was our own sponsored Bill Fish tournament that was kicked off with a dinner. A week later after fishing, there was an awards dinner the following Friday. This event was well attended. We would be celebrating our fifty-fifth year with a dinner and dance on September 19. This dinner would be prepared by the staff commodores of the club. There was a sailboat race for our ladies the last weekend. Our board meeting was good. There were many things in the fire, but we were short on time to get them done. The research and development continued in case the next board was interested in following through. It would now be time to select the new board of directors for the next year. There would be four open seats as directors. It appeared two members would be running for a second term. The vice commodore would need to run for the board if he was interested in being commodore. A director who was a part of the A-Team (accounting team) who had helped get the accounting and office back in order was running for the vice commodore position. He was also the chairperson for our process and procedure committee. This left two seats open for new members. The nominees running were approved by the nominating committee. If this were the case, then the individual running did not have to be present. A spokesperson was allowed to speak in their behalf. This happened with one of the candidates twice. He had missed both the August meeting and the September meeting. He was voted on to the board in his absentee status. Another gentleman, whom I had spoken to about getting on the board, was voted in that evening and was present. I spoke to the second person now a member of the new board about how his interview with the nominating committee had been like. He said he did not have one. Once he admitted he was interested in running, it was an automatic approval. Well, this was not how my process went. I was interviewed twice. At the end of the interviews, I was told I was accepted by that committee to run as a candidate, but if really interested, I would need to campaign. I spoke to the two directors from the board who were on the nominating committee. They also said they did not interview anyone. The process apparently had been dropped to properly interview candidates for these positions. When the nominating committee submits these names as candidates, it is assumed that they were properly interviewed. This process gives them that advantage not to be present during the acceptance process. This person who had not been present was now a director and a past commodore of another yacht club in the harbor. This was a group of electric boat owners who held their meeting in the recreational room of a condominium in the harbor. This person had been a member of our club, but I had never seen him at any of the general meetings in the past. He was also the president for our districts, International Order of the Blue Gavel. His spokesperson happened to be the district director of the IOBG and a past commodore of our club. Yes, I consider them part of what I refer to as the old guard. There was something brewing. I just did not have my finger on the pulse of it. I found it ironic that the three members who interviewed me for a potential member of the board and approved me in 2012 were three gentlemen whom I later started bucking heads with now being the commodore. The first one being our past commodore—El Hefe, as he referred to himself—and the interim director who never got on the board last year. I thought this was classic.

Well, it was now October. We had our dinners, a couple of sailboat races, and bocce ball was in its last month. There was a cruise up to Santa Barbara Harbor and brunch at their yacht club. This was the last cruise of our season. There was our last general meeting and a Halloween social, which seemed to bring the best out of our members in costume. Now came time to select the bridge officers. The commodore was voted in with no challengers. The vice commodore seat had two candidates. They were the new director and a past commodore and the director running for a second term. Both were given the opportunity to address the membership. I knew the turnout would be close on this race. There was a birthday celebration early in the day. Those who attended had quite the party but had failed to return for this important meeting. A vote was taken and the new director won, but not by much. All the inner circle groups pulled together to get one of theirs in position so they could get control. Members who were not present were a little taken back by the outcome of the election, but you needed to be there to cast your vote. The rear commodore position was accepted by an existing board member. This was the board for the next year.

For the record, the $10,000 borrowed from the member in July to complete our payment schedule was returned in mid September. The total cost of the vertical platform lift was paid in full by the memberships donations by the end of October. The project was done on time and on budget, which was estimated at $35,000. Job well done!

Chapter 26

OUR TREASURER WAS GETTING READY for their cruise to Mexico. She had stepped down as of the first of October. I had put in the director who was part of the A-Team as the interim treasurer until the elections. He requested he be replaced the next day after the elections. I notified the commodore of his request and said he needed to fill this position, now that he was the incoming commodore. I said there was a qualified candidate who was young, and she had twenty-five years of experience and had passed her CPA test. She had to change her line of work due to health issues but was willing to step in as the treasurer. I gave him her contact information. On Monday, I was talking to a director on our board. He was saying he had been invited to a dinner at another yacht club member's house. He had never been invited before, but he and his wife accepted the invitation. It was at the spokesperson's house who assisted the new vice commodore in getting voted in. The director had said he had talked to the incoming commodore. He said he would be coming into the area that day that he had a special invite but did not say where. This director and his wife arrived at the home the next evening for dinner. The bar manager was present with his other, the vice commodore and his wife. The commodore entered with his wife and was surprised to see the director present. Out of the ten people present, five were past commodores. The director said the conversation at the table was not too political, but he was not involved in the conversation in the kitchen. He was asked what he knew about the plans of the director who did not get the vice commodore position. He said, "I don't know, why don't you ask him?"

The next day, an e-mail was put out that the host of the dinner was now the treasurer. I was a little surprised. I felt the other person was more qualified and did not have an agenda. I called her that day and asked if the commodore had contacted her. She said yes and said she wanted to have a meeting with him and our bookkeeper. That never happened.

I did go down to the club on Thursday and checked in with the new treasurer. We had a short conversation in the bar lounge. I updated him on his duties as long as I was the commodore. I explained various procedures he would now be responsible for and how they were to be handled since the old treasurer was unable to give him that information due to her departure. The new treasurer was the past commodore from 2005 during the last lease signing. He had no questions. It was apparent they had their own agenda.

It was now November. Now that the new board and bridge were selected, it was time to have the calendar meeting planning out the next year's calendar of events. It was not set in stone but provided some direction into the New Year. I was not required to be there. There was an awards dinner planned for the first Saturday of that month. This was when the commodore had the opportunity to thank those who have made their journey a good one and honor those who worked so hard to make this club great.

I had purchased five cases of wine from a winemaker here in my area. I wanted the bottles without the label because I was having them engraved and a label put on the back commemorating our fifty-fifth year as our yacht club. Our logo was engraved on the front, and the label on the back read: "This blend of three wines from the Santa Ynez Valley embraces the fruits of our labor and celebrating of fifty-five years as our yacht club. It will also christen our future for the next ten years. I would like to thank you for your dedication and support for making this year a memorable one. Bless you. The Commodore."

The label's background was a picture that I had taken in flight over the Santa Barbara Channel of three whales side by side on their migration to Mexico.

The in-house trophies were updated with the names of those that deserved them and were presented to them. It was a fun night for all.

It was November and time to hold the last real board meeting of the year. December's meeting was the commodore taking the board and their spouses to dinner, thanking them for their service.

This dinner was usually paid for by the commodore.

CHAPTER 27

THE MEETING WAS CALLED TO order. The new members of the board were invited by e-mail, but it was stated that they were not to speak or participate. They had next year to be involved. Our meeting was called to order. We got down to business. The bar manager had asked if I would push for a raise for our two bartenders. He would be unable to attend the meeting. I said it would be on the agenda and I would move forward with it. I had asked him two months ago about this item, and he said it could wait. Now it became important at our last meeting. There were many items to be presented, some that would carry over for the next year's board. I would still be a member of that board. Items to be presented for further review included our present POS system (point of sale). Ours was a dinosaur still operating on DOS. The new system linked directly to our QuickBooks accounting program, SOPs (standard operating procedures) that were to support our existing bylaws. I had a template that would make our system more streamlined. We had very few SOPs in place. There were changes to the bylaws that had to be approved before the membership. These items were the most important that should be dealt with in the beginning of the next year. When the treasurer gave his update on the financials, he became engaged in a conversation with the incoming vice commodore. The directors were looking at me. *Why are you letting this happen?* I just nodded, letting them know I was aware of this. A few seconds later, I slammed down the gavel and called point of order. I told the gentlemen to shut up and reminded him this was my meeting, and they were told to not speak. I asked the treasurer if he had anything more pertaining to this meeting. He said yes. He went on to say there was a discovery of a problem in the dinner accounting of cost to profit. When he was done, I asked what he had done about that matter. No answer. "Did I not bring this to your attention in October and you are still talking about it? I have that information and corrections right here. I want to know what has been fixed, not what your problems are. These are your responsibilities, and they were brought to your attention three weeks ago with no action on your part." Same old crap, of disclosure without any resolution. The meeting went well without further interruption. The meeting was called for adjournment.

I was not happy about that situation with the treasurer. I called a director who was the most senior staff commodore and asked for a meeting over dinner. He agreed, and we made a date for the following day. I expressed my disapproval of how the treasurer tried to manipulate the meeting with his interpretation of our financials. After I stated the facts, he agreed that my actions to intervene were valid as commodore. My friend was asked to come down by the bookkeeper and review things for the last time. I approved of this meeting. I offered to drive her down so I could address the treasurer with my concerns. We arrived on Friday as scheduled for 10:00 a.m. I called a director to attend as a witness to what was being said and he would be able to verify our conversation. The treasurer entered the office, and I immediately walked in and asked him to follow me upstairs for the privacy of our meeting. I stated that the director present was there to witness this conversation. I said to the treasurer, "You are under my commodore-ship, and you will abide by what I say." I told him after having a conversation with the bookkeeper that he needed to stop trying to micromanage a situation he had no knowledge of. He said he was working on the commodore's budget. I said, "Then ask for what you need and go upstairs and do whatever. Leave the accounting person alone so she can do her work. To do a budget, all you need is the past two annual profit and loss statements and a current calendar to make a budget. Do you understand?" He tried to explain himself but I said, "What I just said is what you will do. Sign checks when necessary, and follow what you have been told." There was no more conversation. Of course he would not shut up. I just walked out. These people tend to like to hear themselves talk. I then wrote an e-mail to the board and cc'd the new board:

> I would like to bring you up to speed on a recent development. I carefully reviewed our Tuesday board meeting and have moved forward with the following decision. Our treasurer for the new year has been asked to slow his actions down and to focus on one thing at a time. Being involved with an audit, the treasurer and budget committee can be a little confusing where one starts and the other ends. To help provide clarity, the treasurer and I had a meeting where I sat parameters since he is working under my command. Basically as of this time, he is to review receipts and sign checks and observe daily operations without interference to daily operation of the accounting staff. As of now, the audit or discovery is suspended until the audit person is available to take the lead and the treasurer will then assist. When the audit committee was established in April of 2014, it was divided up into three categories. One person doing the financials and the now treasurer and our director followed the others. The audit person on the financials was also involved in developing and accepted the direction I took when our temp agency was terminated on October 31 by the board. At that time, I took control with board approval to get the financials in order and hired and trained a person for the permanent position. This would stabilize the situation creating a transparency that had been previously lacking.
>
> Having a little more than thirty days until the end of the year, this is not the time to be challenging our bookkeeping practice without a valid

examination by one who has been involved in that process.

The treasurer has access to whatever necessary to help develop the commodore's budget for this next year.

For anyone who would like to challenge my authority and decision, I did have a one-on-one meeting with our most senior staff commodore and director who was on the audit committee. He was also present at that meeting. He did agree after I stated the facts that my actions were valid as commodore. I then had a conversation with the treasurer, in which he stated he would abide my request to slow it down. I then informed the staff commodore/judge advocate of my actions. He too agreed that I was within my boundaries of authority.

There can be no changes made to our financials without board approval. Any change will be made in a mock fashion so not to disturb our existing program. You need to remember to change anything, it has to be done so as not to disrupt the history of our accounting system. There will certainly be errors that can be corrected due to placement of explanation, which can be easily be done when a paper trail is verified. The statement of a review by a qualified CPA was presented, all that has been done over the last thirteen months by a Santa Barbara firm. The cost may be a little high, but you get what you pay for, especially when you have to do major housekeeping of several years of accounting without an audit. Everything that was done was done discreetly. Remember, we were going for a ten-year lease extension. If our flaws would have been public, with our catch-up fee debt, it would have seemed more apparent we might not be where we are today. You're welcome.

I believe what the new command should realize is there are five 2015 board members on the 2016 board. The new directors seemed to share the same notion that using common sense and facts are used to make justified decisions. With a change in command, it does not necessarily mean a change is needed. A commodore's term is normally one year, so stability is key to fluidity and forward growth.

If you were to summarize the above, in a cowboy term, we call this "Whoa, Nellie." Let's not get the cart before the horse because you think you have a runaway.

I am not going anywhere. I am a director and the junior staff commodore. Have a fabulous Thanksgiving holiday.

The Commodore

There was the angler's awards dinner the next Saturday night. This was a scampi dinner prepared by volunteers who were involved in the fishing activities of the yacht club. All proceeds went to the White Sea Bass program. This was always a sellout. One of our staff commodores headed this event. He had raffles for prizes that had been donated. There were various awards and trophies presented.

The food was outstanding, and it was just a good time celebrating our angler's programs. With the warm water, the fishing was beyond belief. A live sea horse was found in the sea bass pens when they were being released.

The following Sunday, I received a call from a director with an inquiry from a member asking about the events from the night before. On Monday, I received a call from a member who also had an issue from that evening. I researched each issue as it was presented to me and sent the board of directors my answers to those issues. This was the e-mail:

To the Board of Directors,

The Angler Awards dinner Saturday night was well attended, and the food was outstanding. The host did a great job emceeing his event.

Sunday evening, I received a call from a director that was questioned by a member in regard to employee-member relationship and employee participation in club activities and being recognized as the recipient of club awards.

I was a bit taken back by the questions, but as commodore, it is my duty to find answers to the questions.

After a close review of our bylaws, employee manual, and the house rules by myself and two others, it was decided there is no rule pertaining to these questions.

To find a resolution to the inquiry, I will present the case as I see it.

In reference to members and employees, the employee manual states there can be no close personal relationship between a member and a employee. There is nothing about being a guest of a member. The incident in question was an employee coming to the Annual Awards Dinner. She was a guest of a couple who are members, and they invited her to sit at my table.

I did ask the bookkeeper to attend the Angler Awards dinner. To me, it was so she could meet members and see how events are done and experience it firsthand. This would give her insight to a better understanding of her job. At present, she sits at her desk and goes through the night bags and receipts. Now she understands what it's all about. She was present as a guest, not a date.

I did talk to the member about this, and she assured me that her and her husband's relationship with this employee was strictly on the up and up, nothing sexual. There friendship spans over twenty years, and they think of her as a daughter they never had. Personally I can't believe we have to discuss this, but I did. If there is further inquiry or a change is necessary, that would be in a formal written complaint to be presented to the next board in January. You have my answer to this inquiry, so I can complete my year with a blank slate.

In the case of an employee as a recipient of an award as Sportsman or Woman of the Year, that was the staff commodore of the Angler Awards's decision, and I support his choice. Again, this can be taken up at future board meetings as long as it is not personal.

I received a call on Monday from a disgruntled member about being abused by unnecessary profanity from another member on the cooking crew at the Anglers Dinner. He stated he wanted to make a formal complaint. A formal written complaint would be necessary to move forward. With no board meetings scheduled for the remainder of the year, this would have to go to the next board in January.

My actions at this time were to hear both sides and try settling this manner without board action. Both parties shared a post on the Bridge as port captain. The person registering the complaint will remain as port captain with a new assistant. The other has resigned from his position and has notified the rear commodore. I also asked him to remove himself from any cooking for the rest of the year, and he agreed. I am hoping that my actions will bring this to a close. The member registering the complaint was satisfied by the action taken. No further action is needed.

I have thirty-seven days left in my year as commodore. I hope I can finish this without further incident.

The new board might consider creating a new post to deal with such matters. I would deem that position the petty officer, who would be under the judge advocate to handle such matters before they reach the board. They should also handle the suggestion box in the same manner of order.

I wish you all a good and peaceful Thanksgiving.

Respectfully yours,
The Commodore

CHAPTER 28

I T WAS NOW THANKSGIVING. THE yacht club did have a potluck dinner for those who came. We provided the turkey and ham. The potluck was from the members and their guests. Beyond that, it was time to start decorating the club for the holiday season. Friday would be the tree-lighting event with a light buffet. Sunday was the Jingle Bell Brunch put on by the women's cooking group.

On December 4, I received a call from the office in regards to another member submitting in writing a formal complaint against another member. This was something about an issue that started late in the previous year. It had compounded over the months and had now escalated into this. I did make an effort as I was informed of the trouble brewing to speak to the parties involved without threatening them with disciplinary action. I was hoping that they could work this out. Unfortunately it grew out of proportion because there were too many people involved in that decision-making. This was in regards to the complaint letter I received as the incoming commodore from the in-house women's cooking group. I spoke to the member who had made the complaint; this would have to wait until the new board convened in January. I said I would be on the board but as a director. I would make sure that it was on the agenda at the first board of directors' meeting. She said that she understood and that would be fine with her.

It seemed that the club was falling back into its crazy turmoil again. I had written my final article for our in-house publication. It was usually submitted around the fifteenth of the month before so it could be printed and mailed to arrive at its destination around the first.

I knew the publication was published online. I was waiting for the hard copy before reading it. I was interested in the reaction from members about the article. I was talking to a member and friend and asked what they thought of my last article. They said it really did not make sense so I got online and read what had been published. Well, the article had been butchered. I was aware there were people who edited the publication, but my past articles had never been changed other than corrected for spelling, etc. I did receive a call from the judge advocate about my last article asking if I would accept having two sentences omitted. I said, "OK, is there anything else?" I was told no. Well, I'm sorry they missed the boat with this story, so I decided to publish it myself and sent my complete article as written to thirty members, who then forwarded it to many others.

Well, the incoming commodore got his forwarded copy at the tree-lighting event. He knew I was at the club and asked to speak to me in private. We went to the back balcony. He said, "What is this e-mail you have sent out?"

I said, "It is the article I wrote for our publication. What was printed was not published as it was written. So I took it upon myself to get the real story out."

He said, "You cannot do this. This has to stop."

I said, "Then do not try editing my article, and don't worry—it was my last one." I also reminded him, "I am not a lame duck commodore. I intend to hold the reins until midnight, December 31. Then it is all yours." And I walked away.

CHAPTER 29

MY LAST ARTICLE READ LIKE this:

I would like to thank the women's group for the fabulous dinner they prepared for our Annual Awards dinner. I appreciate all of those who attended. A big thank-you to all who were recognized for their support and service to our Yacht Club. This makes our Yacht Club the special place it is.

You will be receiving your membership renewal for 2016 soon. You will see two small boxes toward the bottom marked Anglers and RBOC. RBOC is a non-profit advocate organization that 84 looks at all legislation governing or being created to govern all recreational boating and waterways. Their money mainly comes from donations from members of yacht clubs and boating and fishing organizations. Your ten-dollar donation helps protect your rights by supporting this group, so please donate. The Angler box is our own fishing group, so please join in the fun.

Since this will be my last article for year, I want to share what it is like to be the commodore.

The first task a new commodore does is bless our fleet at the breakwater and pass out champagne to its captains, later to return to the club for a light lunch and libations. I remember walking up to the past commodore, and I reached out and shook his hand. He said, "It is all yours, don't f—— it up." I just turned away and said to myself, "Sir, that bar has been raised too high for that to happen."

My first order of business was finding out why we were not getting a response about our lease extension. I felt like I was in the movie *The Christmas Carol*. I was being visited by the ghost of the past, the present, and the future of our Yacht Club. It soon became apparent we had a problem. When I presented the catch up fees of $41,200 to the board, the new members were shocked by the news. We were able to come to an agreement with our landlord and then secured our ten-year lease extension.

Once receiving a signed lease agreement, a special meeting was called. On May 8, the purchase, installation, and funding for the chair lift was approved by the membership. After that process was in motion and we were on schedule to meet the completion date, it felt pretty good to be the commodore.

Now having a clearer picture for the future, the rest of the year should be a breeze. Anchor up, full speed ahead. With that thought in mind, I remembered sailing in the Caribbean back in the spring of 1998. It was a perfect day. We were heading in to Punta Gordo, when all of a sudden, I heard the guy at the bow yell, "Boulder ahead!" There was no time to change course, so we hit the boulder with our keel. It seemed as if we had come to a complete stop. Luckily that did not happen. There was damage to the keel, but we did not take on water.

I had similar experience on the first of July, but it came via e-mail. It was from a senior staff commodore, stating my tactics were off-course and that if I professed to be the commodore, "please act like a leader and stop the BS."

I was a little taken back by his comment, as well as to the nature it was delivered. Instead of responding, I once again questioned myself. I got online and Googled "How to be a Commodore?'"

Yahoo's answer results were as follows: "How much is a Commodore 64 system worth? (This is a Computer.) How much should a Commodore 1352 mouse worth? How much should a VN Commodore auto transmission cost to be installed?" There were 1,572 related questions but no answer to my question.

"How to be a Commodore of a Yacht Club" was my next Google search. It was redirected and found *Yacht Club*, "a club that promotes yachting and boating." Thesaurus: "A formal association of people with similar interest." *The Oxford Pocket Addition of the American Dictionary*: "The president of a yacht club."

I looked up *the president*. It said, "the elected head of the Republican government or a person in charge." I thought *Well, if that is true . . .* I looked up "Who is in charge of a Democratic government?" It stated, "a system of government by the whole population through elected representatives."

These explanations seemed a bit convoluted to me.

The next day, I was at our local feed and grain store ordering horse feed. There were some booklets on the counter marked *free*. Apparently, these had been collecting dust for a while. I shuffled through the stack, and one caught my eye. I browsed through it and realized I had found what I was searching for. It seemed to answer my questions when reflecting on my character being challenged.

The title of the manual was "How to Care for Dwarf Hamsters." There was a quote on page 6, stating dwarf hamsters are not cuddly. "Tame dwarf hamsters don't mind being petted, but they also do not like being held for long periods of time. They typically bite when afraid or threatened. With frequent handling and attention, most become tame and good pets. However, it takes time and patience and treats to win their trust."

The moral of this story is if you treat things with respect, you get respect; if not, you might get bitten.

This is a message from your commodore, or as once referred to by another commodore, your *Comode-o-dor*.

When confronted, think first, research it, and pass it off. The main thing is, don't get excited. This makes for the best antidote.

I did look at our SOPs (standard operating procedures) for the commodore, it basically states they oversee several committees. Sorry, cowboys don't do committees. They just get things done.

Have a happy and safe holiday season! Adios, amigas and amigos.

It was time for the last board of directors meeting. It was customary for the commodore to take the board out to dinner for their service and support. It was not mandatory to attend but your choice. In this case, there was another event being held on the Tuesday due to the holiday season. The British brass band would be holding their holiday season concert that evening. I decided to buy gift certificates for dinner from a local restaurant. I put an e-mail stating that they would be receiving a gift certificate for dinner. Two board members were out of town, but those who wanted to could join me. I stated that I would be at that restaurant at six thirty that evening. Anyone else who could not be there were to enjoy this certificate at their leisure.

All but two board members joined me for a wonderful dinner with cocktails and celebrating our year on the board. The other two directors and spouses attended the concert at the yacht club. The directors out of town enjoyed their dinners when they returned. When I saw the past commodore director, he said he had not received his certificate. The next time I saw him, I had a replacement certificate. When I told him I had a replacement he said, "Oh, I finally got mine."

I just nodded and said, "You're welcome."

After that, I was able to finish my year as commodore without further incident!

During my time as vice commodore and commodore, I had reached outside our yacht club. I was seeking comparisons in handling issues such as what I was dealing with. I was questioning myself on what I was seeing and how I might deal with these issues. It was said to me, "I need to refer to your bylaws, SOPs, house rules, and the advice of my judge advocate." That made sense to me. That is what I had been doing.

Later in October as commodore, I received a call from a bridge member of the YRUSC. I was asked if I would consider taking a position on the board. The rear commodore's position was open, and a director position was available. In order to be on this board, you need to have served as a commodore of a yacht club that is a member of this organization. You need to be an active member of that yacht club at the time of serving your position. It was said that the experiences I had endured would make me a good candidate for this organization. I was hesitant to take the position at first. I thought I needed a break. It was explained that these positions were nothing like serving my yacht club. They were in the practice of offering educational seminars on the responsibilities of running a yacht club. Members of the YRUSC have their own facilities, food service, and alcohol permits. These seminars address the laws and responsibilities required to comply with the regulations of a 501.C7 Non Profit. They also have four excellent awards presented to yachtsman, yachtswomen, youth, and all-around excellence.

CHAPTER 30

AFTER A LITTLE DELIBERATION AND witnessing our own election of the bridge I decided to run for the rear commodore seat. I was voted into that position by a majority of our YRUSC membership in November. There were thirty yacht clubs in our membership. I was the first past commodore in our yacht club of fifty-five years to serve on their board.

As the junior staff commodore, it was my decision on the execution of the Change of Watch for the 2016 ceremony. In past years dating back to 2003, the men's cooking group was responsible for the Change of Watch dinner. I was head chef of the dinner in 2013 and 2014. Since this group had imploded in 2014, the resigned USC of that group offered to cook this meal and was responsible for the menu. It was now time for the next Change of Watch. The new commodore was trying to figure out who was responsible. I said with the hiccup with that men's group dissolving, I would say the vice commodore. He was responsible for all dinners. Well, no one was stepping in, and they decided it must be the outgoing commodore, how convenient. Well, me being me, so be it. When you do not know the past, you just make it up as you go into the future. I put together a crew and posted a flyer about the dinner. I would do the meat, and my crew were some friends who had a restaurant who prepared the rest of the meal. I had three club members plate the meal and had four sea cadets with their leader serve and bus the tables. In the official Change of Watch, there is a specific protocol for the seating of the bridge and the junior staff commodore.

Dining tables were arranged for the dinner. Once the ceremony was called, it was the judge advocate who was the master of ceremonies. He ran the show. I would be called up and introduced as the outgoing commodore. A gift was presented to me, and the new commodore was introduced. We shook hands, and I sat down. I was done for the night. At that point, the commodore addressed the membership and then introduced his bridge officers and board members. I asked that the judge advocate give the oath office to the board members all at once and the bridge officers one at time, starting with the rear commodore and up. I had never seen this done at our club before. I thought it was an important way to start the year.

It was the day of the dinner. All was going well. The meat had been prepped, and everything else for this meal was ready. We packed up and headed for the yacht club early so the food could be cooked and the rest assembled. It was a light rain that evening. We were all done with the food prep other than the final finish for the dinner when served. The dining room looked amazing. It was now time for me to walk away from cooking and get dressed for the evening. I went outside to my car. I then realized I had loaded everything necessary but my shoes and clothes. I scrambled around for a white shirt and tie. That was easy. I had no blue blazer. The new vice commodore entered the building. I asked if he might have one I could borrow, while explaining we had the dinner, but in the confusion, I left my clothes at the ranch, which was too far away. He returned with a blazer. He was around the same height but with a much heavier build than I. It drooped over me, but I had a blazer with blue jeans and cowboy boots. Not exactly standard issue, but it was going to have to do. I guess I was taking the outgoing commodore title literally.

Change of Watch Dinner
January 9th 7:00 pm

Panzella Salad Crusty Bread, Tomatoes
Goat Chesse, Pickled Onions, Green Beans, Basil,
Balsamic Vinaigrette.
Smoked Pork Loin or Chicken on request, Green Chile
Sweet Potatoe Mash, Braised Brussel Sprouts with
Bacon. Chocolate Spoon Bread with Chocolate
Garnache. Vanilla Ice Cream

Music by DJ Jim Cubberly who played at our Annivesary dinner $20.00 75 Limit

The dinner was served, and it was excellent. The service was great. It was now time for the ceremony to begin. The judge advocate took the microphone and introduced himself and acknowledged the membership for their presence. I was asked to come up to the podium. I had a few words to say. I was then given a gift from the club for my service as the commodore. It was a bronze statue of a stallion. I made sure by turning it over to make sure it was still intact.

The plaque on the base read, "To the Commodore 2015. We thank you for your guidance by securing our future with our lease and by lifting our spirits with the new elevator." It was beautiful. I had arranged for the chaplain to present me a gift from my departed commodores. She had requested I receive something special, so it was only fitting that the chaplain be the presenter. No one was aware of this exchange being done. I had quietly given this to him to review and read the inscription so he might have a few words to say in its behalf. The chaplain presented me with a blue felt box and said a few words before I opened it. Of course, I knew what it was and what it said. I had ordered it after Sally's passing. It had actually got lost in delivery and had to be replaced by the maker in Montana, who was later reimbursed by UPS. I opened the box and pulled out a big Western belt buckle, like those given at rodeo competitions. It was a beautiful silver buckle with bronze inlay with the yacht club's name on top and "Commodore 2015" on the bottom.

Our burgee was mounted in the center. There were a few words engraved on the back. It was my name and in appreciation for righting the bull.

CHAPTER 31

FTER THE APPLAUSE FROM THE membership, I was excused. The commodore was introduced, and the ceremony continued. Later the board and bridge members were introduced and sworn in under oath by the judge advocate. After that, they were excused. The past commodores were asked to rise and come up to the front. I was asked to join them. I had been asked a week before by a past commodore if I would accept being inducted in the International Order of the Blue Gavel. He said he would be the officer performing the induction ceremony. I agreed. After being given the induction, I was asked if I would abide to their code of ethics. I said yes and I was sworn in. After that, the past commodores passed by me shaking my hand, welcoming me into their order. The ceremony ended, and the band started playing. Nice evening. When I went into the bar, I was asked by someone, "Would you really wear the buckle?"

I said, "Sure, it will be a conversation piece."

If asked, I would say, "Do you want a six-pack or the twenty-four-pack version you are buying?" It was a hell of a ride!

It was time for the first board meeting of the year. The commodore called the meeting to order. The meeting continued as the agenda read. I disclosed the fact that we had established a relationship with a CPA firm while doing the redevelopment of the accounting. I made a motion we should continue with this firm to complete our tax year of 2015. It was seconded by a majority vote in favor to keep continuity to what had been accomplished at this time. The treasurer also agreed, saying this was a relief for him. Well, that did not happen. The treasurer hired a different firm to do the taxes. He had also done exactly what I said not to do. "Do not change the accounting system without a mock review and board approval." This was why you do not have past commodores involved in a process that needs board approval. It just proves they do what they want. They see no need to ask for approval. There was a closed session called at the end to present the complaint from December. A brief recess was called before the meeting so people could be excused who were not board members. The meeting was called to order, and the commodore presented the complaint from the member against another. The complaint was about the conduct of another member's actions through the year, which brought this to a boiling point. I was aware of these events as they unfolded. I did try to intervene without creating a disturbance.

Unfortunately, there became too many people's opinions involved for any kind of solution. Instead it got ugly and was pushed to the board. We could thank the commodore for opening the wound by asking the member the complaint was about to be the yacht club's secretary. She accepted this at first, but when the dam burst, she was asked to decline. The board's decision was to write a letter to both parties. It was stated that you had to get along. This type of behavior could not continue.

I wrote a breakdown of the incidents in question and what brought all this to a head. But this person being asked to represent our club as a member of the board as secretary unraveled everything I had done to settle this quietly. I did explain some of the details to the board but was not adding credence to the matter. So the easy way out was to write the letters to those members. The practice was the secretary and judge advocate drafted the letter for approval and then it was sent to the members involved. They would have thirty days to respond if not in agreement to the settlement. The member who submitted the complaint resigned from the club. The other member remained a regular member. The letters sent out were not done by this process, instead directly from the commodore.

I stated I had another matter to discuss since we were in a closed session. This shocked the bridge members. This matter pertained to the selection of the treasurer position. I wanted the board to be aware of what had transpired in this choice. I had typed up the hold process of what did happen but introduced the fact that the most qualified person should have been given the opportunity to be interviewed for the benefit of what was best for the interest of the club. I had that person come to the regular meeting earlier to be introduced and talk about her view of our bookkeeping process. I had introduced her to our bookkeeper and reviewed a little of our accounting at my request. Afterward, she felt she could be beneficial in the treasurer position to assist the accounting of our business. She had twenty-five years of experience and had passed the CPA test. She had taken a change in her career due to some health issues. With my dealings with the present treasurer, I was only offering a look at the choice and how they were made. The commodore did not follow through with her request for a meeting with the bookkeeper and him for an interview. Instead, he was invited to a dinner with some members in which the outcome became treasurer, the host of that dinner. Just thought those who were not present now knew.

This was far from illegal, just a little favoritism that might not be in the best interest of the club. This was the gist of my question to the board: "Was this acceptable behavior?" When the board members were reading this, you could have heard a pin fall. The floor was carpeted. Once it seemed everyone had reviewed my findings. The vice commodore said my name and stated that I had been disruptive since the elections of the bridge and he wanted it stopped. A new director who had been a member of our club for nine months started viewing his opinion that as junior staff commodore and serving as rear commodore of another organization, I should not be allowed to be a voting member of the board. I said, "You are absolutely right." The YRUSC was reviewing the fact that a junior staff commodore should not serve their second year as a director. It could be considered they could still be pushing their own agenda.

In my review, I finished, stating I had been inducted in the International Order of the Blue Gavel. I will share that oath with you:

> [My name], do you agree to continue to work
> for the best interest of your club by advising

and counseling with active officers of the club without in any way usurping their authority and responsibility? Do you agree to continue to participate in affairs of the club as an active member and to encourage others to do the same? Do you further agree to promote the highest standards of sportsmanship and seamanship, and by all of this upholding the standing and reputation of your club?

Response: As it has been asked of me, so do I agree.

The director again stated his view. I looked around at the directors and said that I would be happy to step down as a director. That same director said that the board would be working on that change in the bylaws along with a few others and thought I should wait. I stood up and said, "If there is no further comment on this subject, I make a motion to adjourn." It was seconded. I then stated that I would be resigning immediately. I left the room.

The reason I wanted to recite the oath is that the vice commodore had already been a commodore and was serving as the president of the IOBG. The treasurer was also a past commodore serving as our district director of the IOBG. I personally found this disturbing, only giving credence to the desires of the old guard wanting control. I was just challenging this matter.

There was a general meeting that Friday. It was the first one of the year. Before that meeting, another director who was the one who did not receive the votes for vice commodore submitted his resignation via e-mail. I came down that evening for that meeting but could not find any reason to enter the room. I did listen to their explanation to these events. I did hear comment being made by the treasurer in his reports that could be considered false about the condition of the financials, but this did alarm some members. I just stayed long enough to be seen, not heard.

There, off and running!

It seemed some of our momentum had gotten lost. How was it possible to take charge of a command without an exchange of procedure? The bridge had no clue of what had happened in the past two years. They were never engaged with the internal works of the club. This could be a struggle. I did say to the commodore that I wanted him to succeed and I was available if he had questions. He declined. He had his own group that was guiding his light.

I was busy attending opening days once again but as the rear commodore of the YRUSC. I had just come back from a day in Marina Del Rey attending four opening days. I was spending the night on my boat to return for three more on Sunday. There was a dinner that night at the club celebrating Saint Patrick's. I came in a little later so as not to disturb anyone. I walked up to the bar and ordered a glass of wine and sat at the comer of the bar. The bartender said it had been a trying evening. She said she was very upset with the evening events and was thinking of attending the board meeting on the following Tuesday and address the board with the issues she was dealing with. I explained that in an open meeting, you have to be careful of what you say if it is about a person. It might have to be discussed in a closed session for the privacy of those involved. She said she had not made up her mind yet, but she was not a happy camper. She did say that the bar manager was made aware of the issues and of her intent to take it to the board.

I excused myself and got some rest before going down to the opening days the next morning. After I had finished my duties, I drove up the Pacific Coast Highway and stopped by the club. I knew she was working, so I wanted to check in on how she was doing from the craziness of the night before. She was still thinking of attending the meeting. I told her she might have a discussion with a director before going and clearing her mind of the event. I said I would meet her along with the director if she was truly prepared to address the board. I left and headed home to the ranch.

Chapter 32

WE CHECKED IN ON MONDAY. She said she was definitely going to the board meeting. I asked if I could set up a meeting with a director and we would have a conversation of the dos and don'ts. She agreed to meet before the meeting at a local harbor restaurant. The advice was to stay focused on the problem, not the people. The bar manager said he was attending. This was not in her behalf but his. I decided to join her in the audience. Club members are allowed to attend board meetings but cannot speak unless on the agenda The bartender did talk with another board member about getting her on the agenda, which she did. We arrived at the meeting and sat down. I was not sitting next to her. The bar manager came in and sat down further behind her. The meeting was called to order. The usual happened, and they tried addressing the people who have requested to be on the agenda first. That way the business could be handled, and they could return to their business.

The bartender was called to speak first. She started explaining her problem. First of all, no one was aware of the procedures that she as a bartender had been instructed to abide by. With that being said, she got caught in the middle while explaining to a member what she had been instructed to do as the bartender and ended up getting attitude from that member and then another. She did not appreciate walking into this type of environment. It was perceived to be hostile. Unfortunately, she went on to speak about the event that happened and then said the names of those involved. This went on for at least ten or more minutes before she was stopped. She was told by the judge advocate that if she wanted to make a written formal statement, it should be submitted at the next board meeting and discussed in a closed session by the board. She said, "I am just making a point—things are out of order. I have no intention of making a formal complaint but I was threatened to have one brought against me. That is why I am here now."

The vice commodore spoke up and thanked her for bringing this to their attention and they would be handling it. The bar manager chimed in on something related to that night, but it was his discovery. The bartender brought this other issue to his attention. She was done and was walking out. I was there to let the secretary and board know what I had going for opening day—band, music for entertainment, etc. I had already filled the secretary in before the meeting started, so I would not have to wait to address the board later in their meeting. When the bartender left, I followed her out. I wanted to get her opinion of how she believed it went. I had been an employer before. You do not let your people stray too far away if they have voiced an opinion or have been hurt on the job. At least they know you are interested in solving a problem. It is called *communication*, not letting this continue or to be held against you. After leaving and going our own ways, a discussion started about where I had gone and why I had left with the bartender and not returned. I was supposed to be updating the board about opening day. The secretary failed to say she had talked to me and already had that information. She and I were directly responsible for the opening day outdoor ceremony. Well then, the rumors started.

There were club members present when the bartender was talking. The commodore or judge advocate should have intervened much sooner. This was not a good thing. That presentation did leak out, starting a whole other problem. It was under wraps but brewing in the air. The confusion that created this presentation did not stop. The board did make some procedural decisions with the help of another committee but again failed to inform those of the change, and the problem persisted. The bartenders were not there to enforce the rules. That was up to the board, bar manager, and bridge to properly implement them so there were no problems. This was a simple request to get things under control.

What was frustrating to me while listening was the process that had been used to monitor and control this matter was lost in the transition. The process was explained to the incoming treasurer, which had been handled from the office through the treasurer, stopped working by him, not following the directions given. A change is not the problem. The problem is the change was not backed with action to make a smooth transition to be followed up by anyone of authority.

The next board meeting, it was obvious that this discussion with the board that night pinpointing a problem excluding the characters was about to change course. It was then said that a formal complaint was being made by a member who was named in the discussion from the previous meeting. And a second person who was named was attending as a witness.

Unfortunately, no one had taken the time to read the bylaws on handling these matters. A formal complaint needed to be in writing form and submitted to the board. It should then be copied so each member of the board and the secretary had a copy for her records. If there is a support document from another member, it should be in written form and copied for the board members to read. The person registering the complaint was not to attend these meetings to relay their feelings. The board ruled on the findings on these matters in private. The person to whom the complaint is against was notified by registered mail and had seven days to submit in writing their explanation to the complaint against them. The board read both sides and voted whether to sustain or not. The reply from the board was written up by the secretary notifying the persons involved of the decision of the board. Those parties had thirty days to submit an appeal if they so desired. There would be no name-calling or outburst at these closed sessions from club members.

There was another incident that emerged, which backfired and slowed this down to a slow roar and eventually made this disappear.

It was understood that a casual meeting was called for those board members who were available to meet at the club on a Saturday. It was brainstorming session. Out of that session spawned an idea to call for a review of the employees. Meetings were called, and the reviews were held by bridge members only. It was decided that the reviews be considered nondisclosure meetings, that what was said was strictly private. One of these meetings got very personal and out of control. It was referenced as ballistic! At the end, it was once again considered nondisclosure and strictly private. Well, as an employee, you'd feel you have been violated. This document meant nothing. The Whistleblower's act protected employees from any action if their actions were validated. Yes, we had directors' and officers' insurance, but one should know better than to take your club down this road for personal reasons. You were supposed to act like adults.

I found myself worrying on what was going to happen next. I knew there was a board meeting coming up. It felt it was time for me to approach the board and voice my concerns on their direction. I was concerned if this continued, it could be a disaster for the yacht club. After finding out there was a closed session scheduled, I sent an e-mail to the commodore to put me on the agenda in the closed session. The next morning and the day of the meeting, I received a reply. He was asking me, "What is this all about?"

I thought for a moment and replied, "As the junior staff commodore, it might be time to review the board." His reply was "OK." I had cc'd the rest of the board. I drove down and decided to get something to eat. I had another meeting at 7:00 p.m. at the club. I was told the closed session would be after the regular meeting. I was sitting with other members of the club when the judge advocate appeared and asked if I had received his call. I said, "No, I was probably on the road when you called."

He said, "I need to talk to you."

I said, "Fine."

He replied, "I need to order food first. I have a board meeting at 6:30 p.m." After he put his order in, we moved to a more private table. He said, "You made my day a little crazy. The bridge officers are not happy about you addressing the board. I have studied the bylaws, etc. Your last duty was the Change of Watch ceremony. What is this all about?"

I said, "This does go back to the Change of Watch. I am attending this meeting as a member of our club, junior staff commodore and rear commodore of the YRUSC, to voice my concerns and to remind the bridge officers and board that they were all given an oath of office and agreed to abide by it. That's all this is about."

He said that seemed appropriate and should not be in conflict. He said they had a closed meeting concerning misconduct. I knew what he was referring to, and that was why I was doing what I was.

We were in a different area of the club holding our meeting. The board members came in, and one said they were on a recess before the next portion of their meeting. I was assured I would be called in when they were done. Our meeting was adjourned, and I stayed and waited to be called in. At about 9:00 p.m., I was told to come in to their meeting. The commodore informed me that the closed session had been adjourned and they were in regular session. I thanked him. I asked to be able to address the board late and not in the beginning so I would be speaking to them as the board and not in front of other members. "I am here as a member, as junior staff commodore and rear commodore of the YRUSC. As you know, you all took an oath of office at the Change of Watch ceremony in front of the membership. By taking that oath, there is a director's pledge— maybe you have read it, maybe you have not. I have nine copies of the director's orientation to pass out. To simplify finding that pledge, I have taken it and posted in the front. It normally is behind page 25. I have been told this document of thirty-two pages is too much to read. So now that we are all on the same page, thank you for your time. That is all I came to say."

CHAPTER 33

I WAITED THREE HOURS TO SPEAK for three minutes to make a point. The commodore started to go through the paper and said they were out of numerical order. I did not bother to reply. I was later told by a board member when it came time for me to address the board, the bridge officers said no. The board insisted I do, and I did. For whatever good it did, I knew I tried without usurping their authority.

It took the board almost two more months to find a resolution to this. Letters were sent out, again by the commodore and using yacht club stationary.

Another incident occurred between an employee and a member. The truth of the matter was, a member was talking about an issue he had with another member sharing his intent on how to deal with this person. The bartenders said this was not a subject they cared to hear about and to please not talk about it anymore. The next night, this same person appeared at closing. The bartender said, "I am closed out, but if you want something, I can put on your house account." They had one drink. The subject she wanted to avoid hearing the night before was being brought back up.

Again it was stated this was not the kind of thing she wanted to be listening to. "Why don't you finish your drink? I need to go home." They did leave, and she went home.

There was an event at the club the next evening, and that bartender was working. She was quite busy. The person who had been in the night before came up to the bar counter and asked for his tab. She replied, "You do not have one." He was referring to the one from the night before.

He leaned in and said, "Come here." She got closer to his face, and he said, "Why did you turn me in to the cops?"

She said, "I did not." She was so close to his face she was afraid he was going to head-butt her. She then stepped back and said, "What are you talking about?" He said he had been visited by two detectives at his residence later that night after leaving the club. She said, "Give me their names. I will clear myself of that. I did not do it." No one at the bar heard exactly what transpired but you could tell she was rather upset. He left the club after she asked for the detectives' names. She told the bar manager, and he told her to tell the commodore. Nothing was done by those two people. It was not brought to the next board meeting either. She felt threatened and kept watch over her shoulder.

She had a few days off and went to San Diego to visit her son and grandson. Later after returning, there was still no further support from the commodore or bar manager. She did contact the detectives involved, and they assured her she was not the person who contacted them. She already knew that, but she said, "You tell him I had nothing to do with this. I have known this guy a long time—I am not going to rat him out. I just did not want to be involved hearing that conversation, and I stated that." What bothered her was he came into her place of work and basically threatened her.

The employee manual read:

> This Yacht Club is committed to providing a work environment free from violence. This Yacht Club maintains a zero tolerance policy for any acts or threatened acts of violence, including hostile behavior, physical or verbal abuse, or possession or use of weapons of any kind on these premises. Making threats, engaging in threatening behavior and acts of violence against other employees, visitors, guest or other individuals by anyone on these premises are violations of our policy. Should you engage in such acts, you will be subject to disciplinary action, up to and

including, including termination of employment. You may also be subject to other civil or criminal liability.

If you feel you have been subjected to behavior prohibited by this policy or witness or have knowledge of any actions that could be perceived as violent, you should report the incident immediately to your Supervisor and or a Bridge Officer. All complaints will be investigated promptly and appropriate action taken. You may also contact the appropriate law enforcement authorities if you have reason to believe there is an immediate threat to your safety and/or the safety of others. Reports or incidents warranting confidentiality will be handled appropriately and confidentially will be maintained to the extent possible. You will not be retaliated against for reporting, in good faith, any conduct prohibited by this policy.

It seemed as if the best thing to have done was to call this person first, state your policies on these matters, and request that an apology on the situation would be warranted since this was not the person who notified the authorities. The bartender was feeling threatened by his behavior as well as him accusing her of this act.

The bartender did call this member and leave a message in regards for the names of the detectives with no response. She also sent a text message requesting the same, with no reply.

After a period of two months, she requested an update on the incident in writing and submitted it to the board. There was no reply. What did happen with her written statement was it was sent to the person as a complaint. The response was resigning as a member and making the statement, "Why did it take you so long to respond to this?"

The board's actions did not bring closure to this event for the bartender. Instead it would seem more she was used as a scapegoat and was still looking over her shoulder.

Well, some things never change. It was time for me to focus on my own things. I was not on the board.

My last duty as the junior staff commodore was the anniversary dinner in September with the assistance of other past commodores of the club. I invited one past commodore and his friend who was a past commodore of another club. I invited a past commodore of another club in the harbor to join us in the kitchen to prepare the meal. I had three members of the club do the serving. Some of the past commodores inquired about their involvement. I said, "You can sit this one out. You all deserve a break, so enjoy the evening. This is not protocol, but it is my dinner, and I will cook with whom I want." It happened that one of my cooks had taken a nasty fall the week before and was unable to help. The dinner was well received, and they all danced their shoes off.

The September elections for the board were held. There were four seats available, and those positions were filled.

The October elections were held for the bridge. The vice commodore now became the commodore. The vice commodore position was filled by an existing director. The rear commodore did not seek a second term on the board. A new director took the rear commodore's position. One director resigned and was replaced. The junior staff commodore had one more year. The bylaw pertaining to this change was approved by the membership, so a new director was voted in that evening. The board consisted of three remaining members, one voted in for a second term and six new directors. Head them up and move them out, forward ho.

This year's activities were pretty much a repeat from the year before. I was interested in sharing the issues facing the club with a new administration.

I am serving as the vice commodore for the YRUSC for 2017. My main task is the commodore's cruise to Catalina Island in July. If I remain with this organization, the next position is the commodore, who is in charge of the officers and directors seminars. You can bet that will be most interesting and thorough in scope.

It is only politics, people, only politics. Happy trails until we meet again!

The Commodore

We stole
the Eagle from the Air
Force, the anchor from the
Navy, the Rope from the Army,
and on the seventh day
when God rested,
we overran his
perimeter and stole
the Globe and have
been running
the show
ever since.

UNITED STATES MARINES

ABOUT THE AUTHOR

D AVID WARDLOW WAS BORN THE son of Ila Mae and Louis Melvin Wardlow at Fort Meade, Maryland. Lou was career army. This branded him an army brat with no particular place to call home. Moving seemed a pastime, always having to adjust to a new environment: Fort Meade, Maryland; Leavenworth, Kansas; Kaiserslautern, Germany; Lawton, Oklahoma; Aschaffenburg, Germany; El Paso, Texas; and finishing high school in Topeka, Kansas. Then he enlisted in the United States Marine Corps. On to Camp Pendleton; Okinawa, Mount Fuji, Japan; and Vietnam. He returned to San Diego by ship and was discharged after three years.

Before serving in the armed forces, becoming a veterinarian or maybe a lawyer seeking the truth was on his agenda.

After returning in country and being treated like an alien in his own country, things changed. Finally, he found solace by becoming invisible as that of the army brat and not standing out.

He did not make a diary. He has come to realize that his two dark brown eyes are connected to his personal flash drive.

He does not have any tattoos to reflect his feelings or memories, or piercings to make a statement. He does have scars from his journey, which are hidden so as to not bring attention.

This story is David's attempt to share a short part of the journey which could not have happened without walking the path of his life.

So, in the end, it is not about him; it is about you, so rock on!

CPSIA information can be obtained
at www.ICGtesting.com
Printed in the USA
FSOW02n0539111217
41831FS